DATE DUE	
~~MAY 1 9 1998~~	

One Hundred
ENGLISH
FOLKSONGS

One Hundred
ENGLISH
FOLKSONGS

Edited by
Cecil J. Sharp

For Medium Voice

Dover Publications, Inc., New York

Published in Canada by General Publishing Company, Ltd., 30 Lesmill Road, Don Mills, Toronto, Ontario.
Published in the United Kingdom by Constable and Company, Ltd., 10 Orange Street, London WC 2.

This Dover edition, first published in 1975, is an unabridged and unaltered republication of the work originally published by the Oliver Ditson Company, Boston, in 1916, in this series "The Musicians Library." The present edition is published by special arrangement with the Theodore Presser Company, Bryn Mawr, Pennsylvania.

International Standard Book Number: 0-486-23192-5
Library of Congress Catalog Card Number: 75-12133

Manufactured in the United States of America
Dover Publications, Inc.
180 Varick Street
New York, N.Y. 10014

TO
Mrs. JAMES JACKSON STORROW

CONTENTS

CONTENTS

CONTENTS

INDEX

INDEX

Cecil J Sharp.

ONE HUNDRED ENGLISH FOLKSONGS

THE first serious and sustained attempt to collect the traditional songs of the English peasantry was made by the Rev. S. Baring-Gould some thirty years ago in the West of England. It is true that the Rev. J. Broadwood had made a small collection of Sussex songs and published them privately among his friends as far back as 1843, and that Miss Mason's *Nursery Rhymes and Country Songs* (1877) and *Northumbrian Minstrelsy* (1882) had both previously been given to the public; nevertheless, the issue in 1889 of the First Part of *Songs and Ballads of the West* marked, I think, the real starting-point of the movement, which has had for its aim the systematic collection and publication of the folk-music of England. Prior to that date the knowledge that folksongs existed in this country was confined to very few, and it was popularly assumed that the English peasant was the only one of his class in Europe who had failed to express himself spontaneously in song and dance. How, in the face of the facts which have since been brought to light, such an amazing misconception could have obtained credence and escaped disproof is an enigma which has never been properly solved. Happily, this grotesque error was exposed before it was too late to make amends for the contemptuous neglect with which our predecessors had treated their national musical heritage. A few years later, with the passing of the last survivors of the peasant class, it would have been quite impossible to have recovered anything of real value, and the products of a great peasant art would have been irrevocably lost. It may be thought that, owing to the late hour at which the interest in our folk-music came ultimately to be aroused, it is but a shrunken harvest that has been garnered. But I do not think this is so. That the postponement has added very materially to the difficulties of the collector — by compelling him, for instance, to take down his songs from aged and quavering throats instead of from young, fresh-voiced sing-

ers — is, of course, true enough. Nevertheless, I do not think that this has appreciably affected either the quality or the abundance of the recoveries. Indeed, our belated conversion has even had some actual advantages. For the investigations have thereby come to be made at a period when the scientific spirit is abroad, and consequently the work has been conducted with thoroughness, accuracy, and honesty of purpose. And this is scarcely the way in which it would have been done a century or more ago. For the 18th century musician had other notions, and was little disposed to trouble himself with ethical considerations where the collecting of the people's music was concerned. Fortunately, the present day collector has set up a very different standard, and has realized that his first and chief obligation is to record just what he hears, no more and no less, and that the æsthetic as well as the scientific value of his work depends wholly upon the truthfulness and accuracy of his transcriptions. And if the investigations have throughout been conducted in this spirit — and it is a claim that may, I think, justly be made — this is owing in no small degree to the influence exercised by the Folk Song Society (founded in 1898) and the example which, by means of its *Journal*, it has set to collectors.

There are two theories respecting the origin of the folksong. Some hold that folksongs were composed in the past by individuals, just like other songs, and have been handed down to us more or less *in*-correctly by oral tradition; that they were the fashionable and popular songs of a bygone day, the compositions of skilled musicians, which found their way into the country villages and remote neighborhoods where, although long forgotten in the towns and cities of their origin, they had since been preserved. To put it in another way, the folksong, it is contended, is not a genuine wild flower, but, in the jargon of the botanist, a "garden-escape."

The opponents of this school, however, impressed by the fact that the essential characteristics of the folksong—its freshness, spontaneity, naturalness, and unconventionality—are the very qualities which are conspicuously absent from the popular song-music of the past, maintain that folksongs are the products not of the individual, but of a people or community, and that we are indebted to the process of oral tradition not merely for preserving them, but for moulding, developing, and, in a sense, creating them as well.

This is not the occasion to enter into a lengthy discussion upon an abstruse and highly controversial question of this sort. Suffice it to say that the writer is a stout upholder of the communal theory of origin; that he believes that the nature of the folksong and its history can be satisfactorily explained only on that hypothesis; that the most typical qualities of the folksong have been laboriously acquired during its journey down the ages, in the course of which its individual angles and irregularities have been rubbed and smoothed away, just as the pebble on the seashore has been rounded by the action of the waves; that the suggestions, unconsciously made by individual singers, have at every stage of the evolution of the folksong been weighed and tested by the community, and accepted or rejected by their verdict; and that the life history of the folksong has been one of continuous growth and development, always tending to approximate to a form which should be at once congenial to the taste of the community and expressive of its feelings, aspirations, and ideals.

The careful preservation of its folk-music is to a nation a matter of the highest import. Art, like language, is but a method of human expression, due to the development and specialization of qualities that are natural and inborn. If, therefore, it is to fulfil this function efficiently, it must never be divorced from, but must always faithfully reflect, those qualities which are peculiar to the nation from which it proceeds. A nation's music, for instance, must, at every stage of its development, be closely related to those sponta-

neous musical utterances which are the outcome of a purely natural instinct, and which proceed, it will always be found, from those of the community who are least affected by extraneous educational influences—that is, from the folk. The penalty that must inevitably be paid when this principle is ignored is well exemplified by the vicissitudes through which music in England passed after the death of Purcell. Prior to the Restoration, musical England held a proud and foremost position among the nations of Europe, a preëminence, however, which it completely lost in the two following centuries, and has never since regained. This very remarkable change was clearly brought about by, or at any rate synchronized with, the open disparagement—at first by the educated classes, and later on by the musicians themselves—of our native music, and the corresponding exaltation of all that was of foreign manufacture. In other words, music in England, which had hitherto been distinctively and demonstrably English in character, fell from its high pedestal immediately it became divorced from the national tradition.

The collection and preservation of our folk-music, whatever else it has done, has at least restored the Englishman's confidence in the inherent ability of his nation to produce great music. Adverse conditions, political, economic, sociological, or what not, may for a time prevent him from making the fullest use of his national inheritance, and postpone the establishment of a distinctive school of music worthy of the tradition of his country; yet, sooner or later, given favorable conditions, English music will assuredly be reborn and once again assume that position which it held before the Restoration.

The greatest care has been exercised in the selection of the songs for this volume, in order that the collection may be thoroughly representative of the subject and contain one or more examples of each of the chief types of English folksong. With this end in view, it has been found necessary to limit the selection to folksongs proper, and to exclude carols, sea-chanteys, children's games, nursery songs, etc.

It will be seen that more than half of the tunes here presented are cast in one or other of the ancient diatonic modes (excluding the major, or " Ionian "), the forerunners of our modern scales. Hitherto, musicians have regarded these modes as relics of a bygone era, which were employed in the early days of the history of music in default of something better, but were eventually discarded (*circa* 1600) in favor of a scale-system better suited to modern requirements. But the diatonic mode is the natural idiom of the English peasant, not one, be it noted, originally acquired from without, but one which he evolved from his own instinct. That the mode has always been, and is still, his natural vehicle of melodic expression, and that it should not, therefore, be regarded in any way as evidence of antiquity, is shown by the manner in which the folksinger will frequently translate into one or other of the modes the "composed" songs which he takes into his repertory. The modal character of so many folksongs has no doubt brought this question very prominently before musicians. For here we have scores of melodies which, although cast in scales long since discarded by the art-musician, nevertheless throb with the pulse of life and make a strong appeal to modern musical taste and feeling. Manifestly, such tunes as these cannot be quietly dismissed as mediæval survivals and relegated, as such, to the lumber room. They reveal, rather, a new species of melody suggesting many possibilities to the composer of the present day.

The modes commonly used by the English peasant are the Æolian (typified by the white-note scale of A), the Dorian (white-note scale of D), and the Mixolydian (white-note scale of G). The Phrygian (E) and the Lydian (F) he uses but rarely ; a dozen tunes in the former mode and less than half that number in the latter are, perhaps, as many as English collectors have as yet unearthed. Of the songs in this collection, twenty-seven are in the Æolian mode, twenty in the Dorian, and nine in the Mixolydian, while four, though modal, are irregular and cannot be concisely classified.

What form the ideal accompaniment to a folksong should take is a question upon which many divergent views may legitimately be held. With the purist, a simple solution is to dispense with an accompaniment altogether, on the ground that it is an anachronism. But this is surely to handicap the folk-tune needlessly and to its detriment. For just as it takes an artist to appraise the value of a picture out of its frame, so it is only the expert who can extract the full flavor from an unharmonized melody. Musically, we live in a harmonic age, when every one, consciously or subconsciously, thinks in chords; when even the man in the street is under the influence — if only he knew it — of the underlying harmonies of the popular air he is whistling. And herein lies one of the fundamental distinctions between folk and art-song. The former, in its purest form, being the product of those in whom the harmonic sense is dormant, is essentially a non-harmonic tune; whereas the latter, of course, is demonstrably constructed upon a harmonic basis.

If, then, the need of an instrumental setting to the folksong be granted, we have next to consider what is its ideal form; and this, likewise, is largely a matter of individual taste. Sir Charles Stanford, for instance, advocates a frankly modern treatment. "The airs," he says, " are for all time, their dress must vary with the fashion of a fraction of time." Personally, I take a different view — and Sir Charles admits that there are two sides to the question. For it seems to me that of the many distinctive characteristics of the folk-air one of the most vital — at any rate, the one I would least willingly sacrifice — is that which makes it impossible to put a date or assign a period to it, which gives to the folk-air the quality of permanence, makes it impervious to the passage of time, and so enables it to satisfy equally the artistic ideals of every age. Now, if we follow Sir Charles Stanford's advice and frankly decorate our folk-tunes with the fashionable harmonies of the day, we may make very beautiful and attractive music, — as Sir Charles has undoubtedly done, — but we shall effectually rob them of their most characteristic folk-qualities, and thereby convert them into art-songs indistinguishable from the "composed" songs of the day.

Surely, it would be wiser to limit ourselves in our accompaniments to those harmonies which are as independent of "period" as the tunes themselves, for example, those of the diatonic genus, which have formed the basis and been the mainstay of harmonic music throughout its history, and upon which musicians of every age and of every school have, in greater or less degree, depended; and further, seeing that the genuine folk-air never modulates, never wavers from its allegiance to one fixed tonal centre, to avoid modulation, or use it very sparingly. Personally, I have found that it is only by rigidly adhering to these two rules—if I may so call them—that I have been able to preserve the emotional impression which the songs made upon me when sung by the folksingers themselves. This, at any rate, is the theoretic basis upon which the accompaniments in this volume have been constructed.

After what has been said above with regard to the "editing" of folk-music, it is, perhaps, scarcely necessary to remark that the tunes in this volume are presented precisely as they were originally taken down from the lips of the singers, without any alteration whatsoever. Logically, the words should be accorded the same treatment. But this, unhappily, it is not always possible to do. Indeed, it has reluctantly to be confessed that owing to various causes—the doggerel broadside-versions of the songs that have been disseminated throughout the country for the past several centuries; lapse of memory; corruptions arising from the inability of the singer to understand words and phrases which have come to him from other parts of the country; the varying lengths of the corresponding lines of the several stanzas of the same song; the free and unconventional treatment of some of the themes, etc.,—the words of many of the songs are often very corrupt, and sometimes unintelligible. It has therefore been necessary to make alterations in the words of many of the songs in this volume. Although archaic words and expressions have been retained, no attempt has been made to preserve local peculiarities of speech, it being the custom among folksingers to use each his own particular dialect. I have only to add that whenever alterations have been made in the text, the fact is mentioned in the notes.

Before bringing these remarks to a conclusion, it is necessary to say something about the singing of folksongs. Traditionally, folksongs are sung not only without gesture, but with the greatest restraint in the matter of expression; indeed, the folksinger will usually close his eyes and observe an impassive demeanor throughout his performance. All who have heard him sing in this way will, I am confident, bear witness to the extraordinary effectiveness of this unusual mode of execution.

Artistically, then, it will, I think, be found that the most effective treatment to accord to the folksong is to sing it as simply and as straightforwardly as possible, and, while paying the closest attention to the clear enunciation of the words and the preservation of an even, pleasant tone, to forbear, as far as may be, from actively and deliberately attempting to improve it by the introduction of frequent changes of time, crescendos, diminuendoes, and other devices of a like character.

NOTES ON THE SONGS

No. 1. *Henry Martin*

VERSIONS of this ballad, with tunes, are in Mr. Kidson's *Traditional Tunes* (p. 30); in *Songs of the West* (No. 53, 2d ed.); and in the *Journal of the Folk-Song Society* (volume i, p. 162).

The words are on a Catnach broadside; and, in Percy's *Reliques*, there is a long and much edited ballad, called "Sir Andrew Barton," with which, however, the traditional versions have nothing in common.

In *English and Scottish Ballads*, Child prints the versions in *Traditional Tunes* and *Songs of the West*, and gives, in addition, four other sets — one from Motherwell's MS., two traditional copies obtained from residents in the United States, and a Suffolk fragment contributed by Edward Fitzgerald to *Suffolk Notes and Queries* (*Ipswich Journal*, 1877–78).

In these several versions, the hero is variously styled Henry Martin, Robin Hood, Sir Andrew Barton, Andrew Bodee, Andrew Bartin, Henry Burgin, and Roberton.

Child suggests that "the ballad must have sprung from the ashes of 'Sir Andrew Barton' (Percy's *Reliques*), of which name 'Henry Martin' would be no extraordinary corruption." The Rev. S. Baring-Gould, in his note to the ballad in *Songs of the West*, differs from this view and contends that the Percy version is the ballad "as recomposed in the reign of James I, when there was a perfect rage for re-writing the old historical ballads."

I am inclined to agree that the two versions are quite distinct. "Sir Andrew Barton" deals with the final encounter between Barton and the King's ships, in which Andrew Barton's ship is sunk and he himself killed; whereas the traditional versions are concerned with a piratical raid made by Henry Martin upon an English merchantman. It is true that in *Songs of the West*, Henry Martin receives his death wound, but, as Child points out, this incident does not square with the rest of the story and may, therefore, be an interpolation.

Unlike so many so-called historical ballads, this one is really based on fact. In the latter part of the 15th century, a Scottish sea-officer, Andrew Barton, suffered by sea at the hands of the Portuguese, and obtained letters of marque for his two sons to make reprisals upon the trading-ships of Portugal. The brothers, under pretence of searching for Portuguese shipping, levied toll upon English merchant vessels. King Henry VIII accordingly commissioned the Earl of Surrey to rid the seas of the pirates and put an end to their illegal depredations. The earl fitted out two vessels, and gave the command of them to his two sons, Sir Thomas and Sir Edward Howard. They sought out Barton's ships, the *Lion* and the *Union*, fought them, captured them, and carried them in triumph up the river Thames on August 2, 1511.

I have noted down in different parts of England no less than seventeen variants of this ballad, and from the several sets of words so collected the lines in the text — practically unaltered — have been compiled.

The air is in the Dorian mode.

No. 2. *Bruton Town*

THE tune, which is a very striking one, is in the Dorian mode. The singer varied the last phrase of the melody in four different ways (see *English Folk Song: Some Conclusions*, p. 23). For two other versions of this ballad, "Lord Burlington's Sister" and "In Strawberry Town," see the *Journal of the Folk-Song Society* (volume ii, p. 42; volume v, pp. 123-127), where the ballad has received a very searching analysis at the hands of Miss Lucy Broadwood. It will be seen that the story is the same as that of Boccaccio's "Isabella and the Pot of Basil" in the *Decameron*, and of Keats's poem of the same name. It is true that "Bruton Town" breaks off at the wiping of the dead lover's eyes, and omits the gruesome incident of the planting of the head in the flowerpot; yet up to that point the stories are nearly identical. The song was popular with the minstrels of the Middle Ages, and was made use of by

Hans Sachs, who derived his version from "Cento Novelli," a translation of the *Decameron* by Stein-höwel (1482). Hans Sachs names his heroine *Lisabetha* and retains the Italian tradition that Messina was the town where the rich merchant and his family dwelt. It is interesting to observe that this ballad is one of the very few that succeeded in eluding the notice of Professor Child.

The words of both the versions that I have collected were very corrupt, so that the lines given in the text have received some editing. For the original sets the student is referred to the *Journal of the Folk-Song Society*, quoted above.

No. 3. *The Knight and the Shepherd's Daughter*

Two versions of this ballad, under the above title, are in the *Roxburghe Collection* and in Percy's *Reliques*. Percy states that his version is "given from an old black-letter copy with some corrections," and that it was popular in the time of Queen Elizabeth, being usually printed with her picture before it." The fifth verse is quoted in Fletcher's comedy of *The Pilgrim* (1621).

Buchan gives two traditional forms of the ballad, "Earl Richard, the Queen's Brother," and "Earl Lithgow" (volume ii, pp. 81-91, ed. 1828). See also Motherwell's *Minstrelsy* (p. 377); Christie's *Traditional Ballad Airs of Scotland* (volume i, p. 184); and Kinloch's *Ancient Scottish Ballads* (pp. 15 and 25).

Kinloch says: "The Scottish language has given such a playful *naïveté* to these ballads that one would be apt to suppose that version to be the original, were it not that the invariable use of English titles, which are retained in all Scottish copies, betrays the ballad to have emanated from the south, although it has otherwise assumed the character of a northern production."

I have collected several variants of this ballad, four of which may be seen in the *Journal of the Folk-Song Society* (volume v, pp. 86-90). For two other versions see the third volume of the same publication (pp. 222 and 280).

The words in the text have been compiled from the several sets in my possession. With the

exception of the lines in the second stanza, they are printed practically without alteration.

No. 4. *Robin Hood and the Tanner*

THIS was sung to me by a blind man, eighty-two years of age, who told me that he learned it when a lad of ten, but that he had not sung it, or heard it sung, for forty years or more. He varied the several phrases of the tune, which is in the Dorian mode, in a very free and interesting manner (see *English Folk Song: Some Conclusions*, p. 21). I have chosen from these variations those which seemed to me to be the most characteristic. Except for one or two minor alterations, the words are given in the text precisely as they were sung to me.

The Robin Hood ballads, which, centuries ago, were extremely popular (although they were constantly denounced by the authorities), are now but rarely sung by the country folk. Those that have recently been collected are printed in the *Journal of the Folk-Song Society* (volume i, pp. 144 and 247; volume ii, p. 155; volume iii, pp. 61 and 268; and volume v, p. 94).

The words in the text follow with astonishing accuracy the corresponding stanzas of a black-letter broadside, which formerly belonged to Anthony à Wood, and is now preserved in the Bodleian Library. A copy of this broadside is printed in Ritson's *Robin Hood*, by Child (No. 126), and also on two 17th century Garlands. The full title on the black-letter is:

"Robin Hood and the Tanner; or, Robin Hood
"met with his Match. A merry and pleasant
"song relating the gallant and fierce combat
"fought between Arthur Bland, a tanner of Not-
"tingham, and Robin Hood, the greatest and
"noblest archer in England. Tune is, Robin
"Hood and the Stranger."

The first verse runs:

In Nottingham there lives a jolly tanner
With a hey down, down, a down, down,
His name is Arthur-a-Bland,
There is never a squire in Nottinghamshire
Dare bid bold Arthur stand.

Ritson gives a tune which, however, bears no resemblance to the Somerset air, in the text.

Robin Hood is said to have been born in Locksley in Nottinghamshire about 1160, in the reign of Henry II. He was of noble blood, and his real name was Robert Fitzooth, of which Robin Hood is a corruption. He was commonly reputed to have been the Earl of Huntingdon, and it is possible that in the latter years of his life he may have had some right to the title. He led the life of an outlaw in Barnsdale (Yorks), Sherwood (Notts), and in Plompton Park (Cumberland), and gathered round him a large number of retainers. His chief lieutenants were Little John, whose surname is believed to have been Nailor; William Scadlock (Scathelock or Scarlet); George-a-Green, pinder or pound keeper of Wakefield; Much, a miller's son; and Friar Tuck. It is said that he died in 1247, at the age of eighty-seven, at the Kirkleys Nunnery in Yorkshire, whither he had gone to be bled, and where it is supposed that he was treacherously done to death.

The Robin Hood ballads were no doubt founded upon the French *trouvère*-drama, "Le Jeu de Robin et Marion," which, in its turn, was only a dramatized version, largely etiological, of the Nature myth, Robin and Maid Marian being the lineal descendants of the King and Queen of the May-day ceremonies. In this connection it is interesting to note that country singers invariably call "Robin Hood," "Robin o' the 'ood," that is, of the wood.

No. 5. *The Wraggle Taggle Gipsies, O!*

COMPARE this song with "The Gipsy Countess" (*Songs of the West*, No. 50, 2d ed.) and "The Gipsy" (*A Garland of Country Song*, No. 32). A Scottish version of the words is in Ramsay's *Tea-Table Miscellany* (volume iv); see also "Gypsie Laddie," in Herd's *Ancient and Modern Scottish Songs* (volume ii, p. 95, ed. 1791). In Finlay's *Scottish Ballads* (1808), the ballad appears as "Johnnie Faa," and in Chambers's *Picture of Scotland*, a valiant effort is made, after the manner of Scottish commentators, to provide the story with a historical foundation.

The tune is in the Æolian mode. I have noted no less than eighteen variants.

No. 6. *Lord Bateman*

THIS, again, is a very popular ballad with English folksingers, and I have noted down nineteen different versions of it. The singer of the Æolian tune given in the text was the old man who gave me "Robin Hood and the Tanner," and here again he constantly varied his phrases in the several verses of the song (see *English Folk Song: Some Conclusions*, p. 22). The words that he sang were virtually the same as those printed on broadsides by Pitts, Jackson, and others.

For versions of this ballad, with tunes, see *English County Songs* (p. 62); Mr. Kidson's *Traditional Tunes* (p. 32); *Northumbrian Minstrelsy* (p. 64); the *Journal of the Folk-Song Society* (volume i, p. 240; volume iii, pp. 192-200); *Sussex Songs* (p. 43); Kinloch's *Ancient Scottish Ballads* (p. 260 and appendix); *English Folk Songs for Schools* (No. 11); and George Cruikshank's *Loving Ballad of Lord Bateman*.

For words only, see Jamieson's *Popular Ballads* (volume ii, p. 17); Garret's *Newcastle Garlands* (volume i); and the broadsides above mentioned. The ballad is exhaustively analyzed in Child's *English and Scottish Popular Ballads* ("Lord Beichan," No. 53).

The story of Lord Bateman, Beichan, or Bekie, is very similar to the well-known and ancient legend concerning Gilbert Becket, father of Saint Thomas the Martyr. This has suggested to some the derivation of the ballad from the legend; but Child thinks that this is not so, although he admits that the ballad has not come down to us unaffected by the legend. He points out that there is a similar story in the *Gesta Romanorum* (No. 5, Bohn ed.), of about the same age as the Becket legend; that there are beautiful repetitions of the story in the ballads of other nations; and that it has secondary affinities with "Hind Horn." The hero's name, allowing for different spellings and corruptions, is always the same; but the name of the heroine varies. In ten of the twelve copies of the ballad that Child gives she is Susan Pye; in two, Isbel or Essels; and in the remaining two, Sophia, as in the text.

No. 7. *Barbara Ellen*

THERE is no ballad that country singers are more fond of than that of "Barbara Ellen," or "Barbarous Ellen," or "Edelin," as it is usually called. I have taken down as many as twenty-seven variants, almost all of which are in 5-time. For other versions of the tune, see the *Journal of the Folk-Song Society* (volume i, pp. 111 and 265; volume ii, pp. 15-18); Kidson's *Traditional Tunes* (p. 39); Rimbault's *Musical Illustrations to Percy's Reliques* (p. 98); Christie's *Traditional Ballad Airs* (volume i, pp. 86-88); and Joyce's *Ancient Irish Music* (p. 79). The well-known Scottish tune was first printed in 1740. The ballad is in Child's collection, where many versions and notes may be found.

No. 8. *Little Sir Hugh*

VERSIONS of this ballad, with tunes, may be found in Miss Mason's *Nursery Rhymes* (p. 46); Motherwell's *Minstrelsy* (p. 51, tune No. 7); *Journal of the Folk-Song Society* (volume i, p. 264); and in Rimbault's *Musical Illustrations of Percy's Reliques* (pp. 3 and 46). For versions without tunes, see Percy's *Reliques* (volume i, p. 27); Herd's *Scottish Songs* (volume i, p. 157); Jamieson's *Popular Ballads* (volume i, p. 151); *Notes and Queries* (Series I); and Child's *English and Scottish Ballads* (No. 155).

The story of this ballad is closely connected with that of the carols "The Bitter Withy" and "The Holy Well" (see the *Journal of the Folk-Song Society*, volume iv, pp. 35-46).

The events narrated in this ballad were supposed to have taken place in the 13th century. The story is told by a contemporary writer in the *Annals of Waverley*, under the year 1255. Little Sir Hugh was crucified by the Jews in contempt of Christ with various preliminary tortures. To conceal the act from the Christians, the body was thrown into a running stream, but the water immediately ejected it upon dry land. It was then buried, but was found above ground

the next day. As a last resource the body was thrown into a drinking-well; whereupon, the whole place was filled with so brilliant a light and so sweet an odor that it was clear to everybody that there must be something holy in the well. The body was seen floating on the water and, upon its recovery, it was found that the hands and feet were pierced with wounds, the forehead lacerated, etc. The unfortunate Jews were suspected. The King ordered an inquiry. Eighteen Jews confessed, were convicted, and eventually hanged.

A similar tale is told by Matthew Paris (ob. 1259), and in the *Annals of Burton* (13th or 14th century). Halliwell, in his *Ballads and Poems respecting Hugh of Lincoln*, prints an Anglo-French ballad, consisting of ninety-two stanzas, which is believed to have been written at the time of, or soon after, the event. No English ballad has been recovered earlier than the middle of the 18th century.

Bishop Percy rightly concludes "the whole charge to be groundless and malicious." Murders of this sort have been imputed to the Jews for seven hundred and fifty years or more; and similar accusations have been made in Russia and other countries of Eastern Europe even in the 19th century—and as late as 1883. Child sums up the whole matter by saying, "These pretended child-murders, with their horrible consequences, are only a part of a persecution which, with all its moderation, may be rubricated as the most disgraceful chapter in the history of the human race."

I have discovered three other versions of this ballad besides the one in this volume. The words in the text have been compiled from these sources. The singer learned the ballad from her mother, who always sang the first two lines as follows:

> *Do rain, do rain, American corn,*
> *Do rain both great and small.*

Clearly, "American corn" is a corruption of "In merry Lincoln;" and I hazard the guess that the "Mirry-land toune" in Percy's version is but another corruption of the same words.

The tune in the text is a close variant of "To-morrow is St. Valentine's Day" (Chappell's *Popular Music*, p. 227).

No. 9. *Geordie*

FOR other versions with tunes, see *Traditional Tunes* (p. 24); *Folk Songs from the Eastern Counties* (p. 47); *English Traditional Songs and Carols* (p. 32); and *Journal of the Folk-Song Society* (volume i, p. 164; volume ii, pp. 27 and 208; volume iii, p. 191).

The tune here given is modal, and, lacking the sixth of the scale, may be either Dorian or Æolian; it is harmonized as though it were the latter.

Child gives many versions and exhaustive notes.

Buchan (*Ancient Ballads and Songs*, volume i, p. 133) prints a version, "Gight's Lady," and suggests that the ballad "recounts an affair which actually took place in the reign, or rather the minority, of King James VI. Sir George Gordon of Gight had become too familiar with the laird of Bignet's lady, for which the former was imprisoned and likely to lose his life, but for the timely interference of Lady Ann, his lawful spouse, who came to Edinburgh to plead his cause, which she did with success—gained his life, and was rewarded with the loss of her own, by the hand of her ungrateful husband." The version in the text cannot, however, refer to this incident.

Kinloch (*Ancient Scottish Ballads*) agrees that "Geordie" was George Gordon, Earl of Huntly, and that the incident related in the ballad "originated in the factions of the family of Huntly, during the reign of Queen Mary." Motherwell, on the other hand, says that in some copies the hero is named George Luklie. In Ritson's *Northumberland Garland* (1793), the ballad is described as "A lamentable ditty made upon the death of a worthy gentleman, named George Stoole."

James Hogg (*Jacobite Relics*) prints another version, and in the *Straloch Manuscripts* (early 17th century), there is an air entitled "God be wi' thee, Geordie."

The words are on broadsides by Such and others.

No. 10. *Lady Maisry*

FOR other versions of the words only of this ballad, see Motherwell's *Minstrelsy* (p. 71), and Child's *English and Scottish Popular Ballads* (No. 65); and of the words with tunes, the *Journal of the Folk-Song Society* (volume i, p. 43; volume iii, pp. 74 and 304).

In the Scottish ballad, Lady Maisry rejects the Northern lords, who come to woo her, and enters into an illicit connection with an English nobleman, Lord William. During the absence of the latter, the brothers of Lady Maisry discover her secret and make preparations to burn her. She dispatches in hot haste a messenger to apprise Lord William of her danger. He hastens home to find her at the point of death. He swears to avenge her by burning her kinsmen, and

> *The last bonfire that I come to*
> *Myself I will cast in.*

The first part of the story is omitted in this version, while the last four verses recall the ballad of "Lord Lovel," rather than that of "Lady Maisry."

The tune is in the Æolian mode.

No. 11. *The Outlandish Knight*

CHILD, speaking of this ballad (*English and Scottish Ballads*, No. 4), remarks: "Of all the ballads this has perhaps obtained the widest circulation. It is nearly as well known to the southern as to the northern nations of Europe. It has an extraordinary currency in Poland."

This ballad is widely known throughout England, and I have taken it down no less than thirty-six times. Although very few singers could "go through" with it, I have recorded several fairly complete sets of words, from which that given in this book has been compiled. As a rule the versions vary but little, although I have heard only one singer sing the seventh and eighth stanzas of the text. One singer, however, used the word "cropped," instead of the more usual "dropped," in the ninth stanza, and this may have been a reminiscence of the "nettle" theme. None of the printed copies contain these verses except one in the *Roxburghe Collection*, in which the following lines occur:

> *Go fetch the sickle, to crop the nettle,*
> *That grows so near the brim;*
> *For fear it should tangle my golden locks,*
> *Or freckle my milk-white skin.*

The Rev. S. Baring-Gould has collected a similar verse in Devonshire.

As "May Colvin," the ballad appears in Herd's *Scottish Songs* (volume i, p. 153), in Motherwell's *Minstrelsy* (p. 67, tune 24), and in Buchan's *Ancient Ballads and Songs of the North of Scotland* (volume ii, p. 45). Buchan also gives a second version of the ballad entitled "The Gowans sae Gay" (volume i, p. 22). In the latter, the hero appears as an elf-knight, and the catastrophe is brought about by the heroine, Lady Isabel, persuading her false lover to sit down with his head on her knee, when she lulls him to sleep with a charm and stabs him with his own dagger. None of the English versions introduce any supernatural element into the story. They all, however, contain the "parrot" verses.

The expression "outlandish" is generally taken to mean an inhabitant of the debatable territory between the borders of England and Scotland. In other parts of England, however, "outlandish" simply means "foreign," *i.e.*, not belonging to the county or district of the singer.

One singer gave me the first verse as follows:

> *There was a knight, a baron-knight,*
> *A knight of high degree;*
> *This knight he came from the North land,*
> *He came a-courting me.*

Child points out that the ballad has some affinity with "Bluebeard," and, possibly, also with the story of "Judith and Holofernes" in the Apocrypha.

For versions with tunes, see the *Journal of the Folk-Song Society* (volume ii, p. 282; volume iv, pp. 116-123); *Traditional Tunes* (pp. 26 and 172); *English County Songs* (p. 164); and a Border version in *Northumbrian Minstrelsy* (p. 48).

The tune is nearly always in $\frac{6}{8}$ time, and is usually modal. The second air, however, in *Tra-*

ditional Tunes and a variant collected by the Rev. S. Baring-Gould in Devon and printed in *English Folk Songs for Schools*, are both in common measure.

The singer varied his tune, which is in the Dorian mode, in nearly every verse.

No. 12. *The Coasts of High Barbary*

A VERSION of this song, which the Rev. S. Baring-Gould collected in Devonshire, is published in *English Folk Songs for Schools*. I have collected only one other version, the first stanza of which runs thus:

> *Two lofty ships of war from old England set sail;*
> *Blow high, blow low, and so sailed we,*
> *One was the Princess Charlotte and the other the*
>   *Prince of Wales,*
> *A-coming down along the coasts of Barbary.*

The ballad is evidently related to an old broadside sea-song, which Mr. Ashton reproduces in his *Real Sailor Songs*. It is headed "The Sailor's onely Delight, shewing the brave fight between the George-Aloe, the Sweepstake, and certain Frenchmen at sea," and consists of twenty-three stanzas, the first of which runs:

> *The George-Aloe and the Sweepstake, too,*
>   *with hey, with hoe, for and a nony no,*
> *O, they were Merchant men, and bound for Safee*
>   *and alongst the Coast of Barbary.*

Mr. Ashton thinks that the "ballad was probably written in the latter part of the sixteenth century," and he points out that it is quoted in a play, "The Two Noble Kinsmen," written by "the Memorable Worthies, Mr. John Fletcher and Mr. William Shakespeare."

To the six verses which the singer sang to me I have added three others; two from the Devon version (with Mr. Baring-Gould's kind permission), and one—the last one in the text—from the broadside above mentioned.

The third phrase of the tune, which is in the Æolian mode, is not unlike the corresponding phrase of "When Johnny comes Marching Home Again." Compare, also, "Whistle, Daughter, Whistle" (No. 59).

No. 13. *The Cruel Mother*

THE story, which is not quite clear in this version, is of a woman who contracts an illicit alliance with her father's clerk, and secretly gives birth to twin babes "down by the green wood side O." She murders the infants, who afterward appear before her "all dressed in white," that is, as ghosts. They proclaim their identity by calling her " Mother," curse her for her cruelty to them, and say that they live in heaven, but that she will suffer in hell for her misdeeds.

The earliest published form of the ballad is in Herd's *Scottish Songs* (volume ii, p. 237, ed. 1776). Other Scottish versions are given in Motherwell's, Kinloch's, and Buchan's collections; see also "Lady Anne" in Scott's *Minstrelsy*, and "Fine Flowers in the Valley" in Johnson's *Museum* (volume iv, ed. 1792). The tune given in the latter, although quite regular in rhythm, is very similar to the air given here.

Kinloch also quotes a tune which, however, has little or nothing in common with the Mixolydian air in the text.

In the *Percy Papers* there is a version very similar to this one. It begins:

> *There was a duke's daughter lived in York,*
> All alone and alone a,
> *And she fell in love with her father's clarke,*
> Down by the green wood side a.

Child points out that the ballad has affinities with "The Maid and the Palmer," and quotes two Danish ballads which are closely allied to the British song.

Four versions with tunes are printed in the *Journal of the Folk-Song Society* (volume ii, p. 109; volume iii, pp. 70-72), the first one of which was recorded by Miss Esther White, of New Jersey, who writes that "lately she heard it again, sung by a poor 'mountain-white' child in the North Carolina Mountains."

No. 14. *The Golden Vanity*

MANY versions of this ballad have been published with tunes, for example, the *Journal of the Folk-Song Society* (volume i, p. 104; volume ii,

p. 244); *English County Songs* (p. 182); *Songs of the West* (No. 64, 2d ed.); Tozer's *Sailors' Songs and Chanties* (No. 15); *Songs of Sea-Labour* (No. 42), etc.

Child (No. 286) reprints a 17th century broadside version, beginning:

> *Sir Walter Raleigh has built a ship*
> *In the Netherlands,*
> *And it is called the* Sweet Trinity
> *And was taken by the false Gallaly,*
> *Sailing in the Lowlands.*

Mr. Ebsworth, in his introduction to the ballad in the *Roxburghe Ballads* (volume v, p. 418), points out that the selfishness and ingratitude displayed by Raleigh in the ballad agreed with the current estimate of his character.

The ballad is still freely sung by English folksingers, from whom I have noted down twelve different versions.

No. 15. *Lord Thomas of Winesberry*

I HAVE had to omit some of the words which the singer of this version gave me, and to supplement the rest with extracts from the three other variants I have collected. All the tunes that I have noted are of the same straightforward type.

The ballad is very nearly identical with the Scottish ballad of "Lord Thomas of Winesberry," and that is my excuse for appropriating that title. Scottish versions are printed in Buchan's *Ancient Ballads of the North of Scotland* (volume ii, p. 212), and in Kinloch's *Ancient Scottish Ballads* (p. 89). Kinloch makes an attempt to connect the subject of the ballad with "the secret expedition of James V to France, in 1536, in search of a wife," which seems more ingenious than probable. In Buchan's version Thomas is chamberlain to the daughter of the King of France, who wanted none of her riches, as he had

> *. . . thirty ploughs and three:*
> *And four an' twenty bonny breast mills,*
> *All on the water of Dee.*

Under the heading of "Willie o' Winsbury," Child treats the ballad very exhaustively (*English and Scottish Ballads*, No. 100). He gives a version from Motherwell's MS., in which the curious line, "But a fig for all your land," occurs. Shakspere uses the same expression, "A fig for Peter" (2 *Henry VI*, Act ii, Sc. 3).

Five verses of this ballad are given in *Notes and Queries* (Series 5, volume vii, p. 387), "as heard sung years ago by a West Country fisherman." As the late Mr. Hammond noted down more than one version in Dorset, the song has evidently taken root in the West of England, where all my versions were collected.

No. 16. *The Green Wedding*

THE words of this ballad were sung to me to a very poor tune. I have, therefore, taken the liberty of mating them to a fine air which was sung to me to some very boisterous, unprintable words, called "The Boatsman and the Tailor." The occasional substitution of a minor for the major third in a Mixolydian tune is quite a common habit with English folksingers, and several examples of this may be seen in this volume (see Nos. 46, 47, and 53 [second version]); but for the major interval to follow the minor almost immediately is both curious and unusual. Miss Gilchrist has pointed out the close connection between "The Green Wedding" and the Scottish ballad "Katherine Janfarie," or "Jaffray," upon which Scott founded his ballad of "Lochinvar" in *Marmion* (see Child's *English and Scottish Ballads*; Motherwell's *Minstrelsy*; Sidgwick's *Popular Ballads of the Olden Time*; and Scott's *Minstrelsy*, 1st and 3d editions).

In the Scottish ballad, Katherine is wooed first by the Laird of Lauderdale, who wins her consent, and secondly by Lord Lochinvar "out frae the English border," who, however, omitted to avow his love to Katherine "till on her wedding e'en." The rivals meet at the "wedding house" and, in the fight that ensues, Katherine is carried off by her Scottish lover.

Whether our ballad is a corrupt and incomplete version of the Scottish one, it is difficult to say. Although the two have several lines in common, there is something in the plot of "The Green Wedding" which, despite its obscurity,

seems to indicate a motive which is absent from "Katherine Janfarie." The scheme of our story seems to turn upon the dressing in green of both hero and heroine at the wedding feast, but the purpose of their device is not clear. This, however, presented no difficulty to my singer, who, when I asked him why the hero dressed in green, said, "Because, you see, he had told his true-love to dress in green also;" and when I further inquired why he told her to do this, he said, "Because, of course, he was going to put on a green dress himself"—and there was clearly nothing more to be said!

It is just possible, as Miss Gilchrist observes, that the reference to the green dress may be a reminiscence of "Robin Hood and Allan-a-Dale;" or perhaps it has been suggested by the following stanza which occurs in "Katherine Janfarie:"

> *He's ta'en her by the milk-white hand,*
> *And by the grass-green sleeve;*
> *He's mounted her hie behind himsell,*
> *At her kinsmen speir'd na leave.*

No. 17. *The Briery Bush*

THE lines printed in the text are as the singer of this version sang them, with the exception of the last stanza, which I have borrowed from a variant collected elsewhere. For other versions with tunes, see *English County Songs* (p. 112); and the *Journal of the Folk-Song Society* (volume v, pp. 228-235), with a long and exhaustive note.

Under the heading of "The Maid freed from the Gallows," Child (*English and Scottish Ballads*, No. 95) gives several versions and shows that the ballad is very generally known throughout Northern and Southern Europe—nearly fifty versions have been collected in Finland. In the foreign forms of the ballad, the victim usually falls into the hands of corsairs or pirates, who demand ransom, but none of the English versions account in any way for the situation.

Child also quotes another English variant communicated by Dr. Birkbeck Hill in 1890, "as learned forty years before from a schoolfellow who came from the North of Somerset."

This is very much like the version given in the text, the first two lines of the refrain running:

Oh the briers, prickly briers,
Come prick my heart so sore.

The Rev. S. Baring-Gould, in the appendix to Henderson's *Notes on the Folk-Lore of the Northern Counties of England* (p. 333, ed. 1866), gives a Yorkshire story, "The Golden Ball," which concludes with verses very similar to those of "The Briery Bush." A man gives a ball to each of two maidens, with the condition that if either of them loses the ball, she is to be hanged. The younger, while playing, tosses her ball over a park-paling; the ball rolls away over the grass into a house and is seen no more. She is condemned to be hanged, and calls upon her father, mother, etc., for assistance, her lover finally procuring her release by producing the lost ball.

Child quotes a Cornish variant of the same story, communicated to him by Mr. Baring-Gould.

That the ballad is a very ancient one may be inferred from the peculiar form of its construction—sometimes called the "climax of relatives." The same scheme is used in the latter half of "Lord Rendal" (No. 18), and is one that lends itself very readily to improvisation.

No. 18. *Lord Rendal*

THIS ballad is sung very freely from one end of the island to the other, and I have taken it down at least twenty times.

The words given in the text have been compiled from different sets, but none of them have been altered.

One of the earliest printed versions of this ballad is in Johnson's *The Scots Musical Museum* (1787–1803) under the heading "Lord Ronald my Son;" and that is a fragment only. The "Willy Doo" in Buchan's *Ancient Ballads* (1828) is the same song; see also "Portmore" in the same volume.

Sir Walter Scott, in *Minstrelsy of the Scottish Border* (1828), calls it "Lord Randal," and thinks it not impossible "that the ballad may have

originally referred to the death of Thomas Randolph, or Randal, Earl of Murray, nephew to Robert Bruce and governor of Scotland. This great warrior died at Musselburgh, 1332, at the moment when his services were most needed by his country, already threatened by an English army. For this sole reason, perhaps, our historians obstinately impute his death to poison." But, of course, Sir Walter did not know how many countries have the ballad.

A nursery version of the ballad is quoted in Whitelaw's *Book of Scottish Ballads*, under the title, "The Croodlin Doo" (Cooing Dove). Jamieson gives a Suffolk variant, and also a translation of the German version of the same song, called "Grossmutter Schlangenkoechin," that is, Grandmother Adder-cook. The German version is like ours in that it attributes the poisoning to snakes, not toads, which is the Scottish tradition. Kinloch remarks: "Might not the Scots proverbial phrase, 'To gie one frogs instead of fish,' as meaning to substitute what is bad or disagreeable, for expected good, be viewed as allied to the idea of the venomous quality of the toad?" Sir Walter Scott quotes from a manuscript Chronicle of England which describes in quaint language how King John was poisoned by a concoction of toads: "Tho went the monke into a gardene, and fonde a tode therin; and toke her upp, and put hyr in a cuppe, and filled it with good ale, and pryked hyr in every place, in the cuppe, till the venom came out in every place; and brought hitt before the kynge, and knelyd, and said, 'Sir, wassayle; for never in your lyfe dranck ye of such a cuppe.'"

A very beautiful version of the song is given in *A Garland of Country Song*, No. 38. In the note, Mr. Baring-Gould remarks that, not only is the ballad popularly known in England and Ireland, but it has also been noted down in Italy, Germany, Holland, Denmark, Sweden, Hungary, Bohemia, and Iceland. The ballad is exhaustively dealt with by Child.

The West Country expression "spickit and sparkit" means "speckled and blotched."

For other versions with tunes, see the *Journal*

of the Folk-Song Society (volume ii, pp. 29-32; volume iii, p. 43; volume v, pp. 244-248).

No. 19. *Blow away the Morning Dew*

This is a shortened form of "The Baffled Knight, or Lady's Policy" (Percy's *Reliques*). The words beginning "Yonder comes a courteous knight" are preserved in *Deuteromelia*, 1609, and in *Pills to Purge Melancholy* (volume iii, p. 37, ed. 1719). A tune to which this ballad was once sung is to be found in Rimbault's *Music to Reliques of Ancient Poetry*. See also "Blow the winds I ho!" in Bell's *Ballads of the English Peasantry*, and "Blow away ye mountain breezes," in Baring-Gould's *Songs of the West* (No. 25, 2d ed.).

A Scottish version of the words, "Jock Sheep," is given in *The Ballad Book* (Kinloch and Goldsmid, p. 10); and another, "The Abashed Knight," in Buchan's *Ancient Ballads and Songs* (volume ii, p. 131). For other versions, see Child's collection. I have secured thirteen variants, one of which was used as a Capstan Chantey.

No. 20. *The Two Magicians*

This is, I believe, the only copy of this ballad that has as yet been collected in England. The tune, which, of course, is modern, is a variant of one which was used for a series of humorous songs of the "exaggeration" type that was very popular in the 18th and 19th centuries, of which "The Crocodile" (*English County Songs*, p. 184) is an example.

The words were first printed, I believe, in 1828 in Buchan's *Ancient Ballads and Songs* (volume i, p. 24), together with the following comment: "There is a novelty in this legendary ballad very amusing, and it must be very old. I never saw anything in print which had the smallest resemblance to it." It has been necessary to make but one or two small alterations in the words.

Child (*English and Scottish Ballads*, volume i, p. 244) prints Buchan's version and says: "This is a base born cousin of a pretty ballad known all over Southern Europe and elsewhere, and in especially graceful forms in France."

"The French ballad generally begins with a young man's announcing that he has won a mistress, and intends to pay her a visit on Sunday, or to give her an *aubade*. She declines his visit or his music. To avoid him she will turn, *e.g.* into a rose; then he will turn bee and kiss her. She will turn quail; he sportsman and bag her. She will turn carp; he, angler, and catch her. She will turn hare; and he hound. She will turn nun; and he priest and confess her day and night. She will fall sick; he will watch with her or be her doctor She will become a star; he a cloud and muffle her. She will die; he will turn earth into which they will put her, or into Saint Peter, and receive her into Paradise. In the end she says, 'Since you are inevitable, you may as well have me as another;' or more complaisantly, 'Je me donnerai à toi, puisque tu m'aimes tant.'"

The ballad in varying forms is known in Spain, Italy, Roumania, Greece, Moravia, Poland, and Servia. See the chapter on "Magical Transformations and Magical Conflict," in Clouston's *Popular Tales and Fiction*. I believe there is a similar story in the *Arabian Nights' Entertainment*.

No. 21. *The Duke of Bedford*

The singer of this ballad, a native of Sheffield, told me that he learned it from his father, who, in turn, had derived it from his father, and that it was regarded by his relatives as a "family relic" and sung at weddings and other important gatherings. The earlier stanzas of the song are undoubtedly traditional, but some of the later ones (omitted in the text) were, I suspect, added by a recent member of the singer's family, or, possibly, derived from a broadside.

The tune, which is in the Æolian mode, has some affinities with the second strain of "The Cuckoo" (No. 35), an air which is often sung to "High Germany." See also the tune of No. 92 of Joyce's *Ancient Irish Music*.

Three Lincolnshire variants collected by Percy Grainger are printed in the *Journal of the Folk-Song Society* (volume iii, pp. 170-179); while the version in the text is given, with all the words, in the fifth volume of the same publication (p. 79).

Very full notes have been added to these by Miss Lucy Broadwood in an attempt to throw light on the origin of the historical incident upon which the ballad story is founded. Two other versions have been published in *Longman's Magazine* (volume xvii, p. 217, ed. 1890), and in the *Ballad Society's* edition of the *Roxburghe Ballads* (part xv, volume v, ed. 1885).

Professor Child reprinted the first of these in a note upon "The Death of Queen Jane," observing that "one half seemed a plagiarism upon that old ballad," and that the remainder of "The Duke of Bedford" was so "trivial" that he had not attempted to identify this Duke—"any other Duke would probably answer as well." Miss Broadwood has not reached a definite conclusion, but she inclines to the theory that the Duke of the ballad was William De la Pole, first Duke of Suffolk (1396–1450). She admits, however, that there is a good deal of evidence in favour of the Duke of Grafton, son of Charles II, an account of whose death was printed on a broadside, licensed in 1690. She thinks that the ballad given here is probably a mixture of two separate ballads, the more modern of the two (describing hunting) referring to the death of the son of the fourth Duke of Bedford, born in 1739, who was killed by a fall from his horse in 1767. Woburn only came into the possession of the Bedford family after the accession of Edward VI.

The last stanza refers to the popular superstition that the flowing of certain streams, known as "woe-waters," was the presage of coming disaster.

No. 22. *Death and the Lady*
FOR other versions with tunes, see *Journal of the Folk-Song Society* (volume i, p. 169; volume ii, p. 137); *Songs of the West* (No. 99, 2d ed.); *English Traditional Songs and Carols* (p. 40); and Chappell's *Popular Music of the Olden Time* (pp. 164–168).

Chappell points out that this "is one of a series of popular ballads which had their rise from the celebrated *Dance of Death*," and he quotes a very long "Dialogue betwixt an Exciseman and Death" from a copy in the Bagford Collection, dated 1659 (also given in Bell's *Songs of the Peasantry of England*). There is a tune in Henry Carey's *Musical Century* (volume i, p. 53), set to one of the recitatives in "A New Year's Ode." This is headed, "The melody stolen from an old ballad called Death and the Lady." It is this tune which Chappell prints to the words of "Death and the Lady," from *A Guide to Heaven* (1736). The words of this last version are on a broadside by Evans which I am fortunate enough to possess. It is ornamented with a curious old woodcut of a skeleton holding a scythe in one hand and an hour-glass in the other.

No. 23. *The Low, Low Lands of Holland*
ONE of the earliest copies of this ballad is printed in Herd's *Ancient and Modern Scottish Songs* (volume ii, p. 2, ed. 1776). It is also in the *Roxburghe* and *Ebsworth Collections* and in Johnson's *Museum*. The ballad appears also in Garlands, printed about 1760, as "The Sorrowful Lover's Regrate" and "The Maid's Lamentation for the Loss of her True Love," as well as on broadsides of more recent date. See also the *Pedlar's Pack of Ballads* (pp. 23–25); the *Journal of the Folk-Song Society* (volume i, p. 97; volume iii, p. 307); and Dr. Joyce's *Ancient Irish Music* (No. 68).

The "vow" verse occurs in "Bonny Bee Hom," a well-known Scottish ballad (Child, No. 92).

The words in the text are virtually as I took them down from the singer. The tune is partly Mixolydian. The word "box" in the third stanza is used in the old sense, that is "to hurry."

No. 24. *The Unquiet Grave*, or, *Cold Blows the Wind*
THIS ballad, of which I have collected a large number of variants, is widely known and sung by English folksingers. A Scottish version, "Charles Graeme," is in Buchan's *Ancient Ballads and Songs*; while several traditional versions of the words are printed by Child. Compare the ballad of "William and Marjorie" (Motherwell's *Minstrelsy*, p. 186), and versions of the well-known "William and Margaret." For variants

with tunes, see the *Journal of the Folk-Song Society* (volume i, pp. 119 and 192; volume ii, p. 6); *English County Songs* (p. 34); *Songs of the West* (p. 12, 2d ed.); and *English Traditional Songs and Carols* (p. 50). The words of the sixth stanza in the text refer to an ancient belief that a maiden betrothed to a man was pledged to him after his death, and was compelled to follow him into the spirit world unless she was able to perform certain tasks or solve certain riddles that he propounded. In this particular version the position is, of course, reversed, and it is the maiden who lies in the grave. Compare "Scarborough Fair" (No. 74).

No. 25. *The Trees they do grow high*

THE singer varied his tune, which is in the Dorian mode, in a very remarkable way, a good example of the skill with which folksingers will alter their tune to fit various metrical irregularities in the words (see *English Folk Song: Some Conclusions*, p. 25). For versions with tunes, see the *Journal of the Folk-Song Society* (volume i, p. 214; volume ii, pp. 44, 95, 206, and 274); *Songs of the West* (No. 4, 2d ed.); *English Traditional Songs and Carols* (p. 56); Christie's *Traditional Ballad Airs* ("Young Craigston"); and Johnson's *Scots Musical Museum*, volume iv ("Lady Mary Ann"). For some reason or other, Child makes no mention of this ballad. For particulars of the custom of wearing ribands to denote betrothal or marriage, see "Ribands" in Hazlitt's *Dictionary of Faiths and Folk-Lore*.

No. 26. *Lord Lovel*

I DO not know of any publication in which the tune of this ballad is published. I have collected six versions, but only one complete set of words, the one given in the text (with the exception of the last two stanzas). Versions of the words are given in Child (*English and Scottish Ballads*); Bell's *Early Ballads* (p. 134); and Kinloch's *Ancient Scottish Ballads*.

No. 27. *False Lamkin*

UNDER the heading "Lamkin," Child deals very fully with this ballad. There is a tradition in Northumberland that Lamkin and his tower were of that county, and Miss Broadwood says that she has seen what is said to be the original tower close to the little village of Ovingham-on-Tyne, "now a mere shell overgrown with underwood."

For other versions with tunes, see Christie's *Traditional Ballad Airs of Scotland* and the *Journal of the Folk-Song Society* (volume i, p. 212; volume ii, p. 111; volume v, pp. 81-84). The ballad given here was collected in Cambridgeshire, in which county it is still very generally known to folksingers.

No. 28. *Lord Thomas and Fair Ellinor*

THIS, of course, is a very common ballad. The words are on ballad-sheets and in most of the well-known collections, and are fully analyzed in Child's *English and Scottish Ballads*. For versions with tunes, see the *Journal of the Folk-Song Society* (volume ii, pp. 105-108); *English County Songs* (p. 42); Sandys's *Christmas Carols*; *Traditional Tunes* (p. 40); Ritson's *Scottish Songs* (Part iv, p. 228); etc.

The singer assured me that the three lines between the twentieth and twenty-first stanzas were always spoken and never sung. This is the only instance of the kind that I have come across (see *English Folk Song: Some Conclusions*, p. 6).

No. 29. *The Death of Queen Jane*

FOR other versions see Child (No. 170) and the *Journal of the Folk-Song Society* (volume ii, p. 221; volume iii, p. 67).

Queen Jane Seymour gave birth to Prince Edward, afterwards Edward VI, on October 12, 1537, and died twelve days later. There is no evidence that her death was brought about in the way narrated in the ballad.

No. 30. *Farewell, Nancy*

VERSIONS with tunes are given in the *Journal of the Folk-Song Society* (volume i, p. 130; volume ii, pp. 99 and 298); and in Joyce's *Ancient Irish Music* (No. 93).

See also "William and Nancy's parting," in Garret's *Newcastle Garlands* (volume ii).

The tune, a remarkably fine one, is in the Æolian mode, and was sung to me by a woman, seventy-four years of age.

No. 31. *Sweet Kitty*

THE tune, which is in the Dorian mode, was used in Mr. Granville Barker's production of Hardy's "Dynasts," being set to the words, "My Love's gone a-fighting." The words, which are related to those of "Brimbledon Fair" (No. 75), have been compiled from several versions that I have collected.

No. 32. *The Crystal Spring*

I HAVE no variants of this song, nor have I been able to find it on ballad-sheets or in any published collection. I believe the tune to be a genuine folk-melody, though the sequence in the first phrase is unusual. On the other hand, the middle cadence on the third degree of the scale (thus avoiding a dominant modulation) is very characteristic of the folk-tune proper.

No. 33. *The Seeds of Love*

THIS song, which is known to the peasant-folk all over England, is a modernized version of "The Sprig of Thyme," the next number in this collection. According to Whittaker's *History of the Parish of Whalley*, the words were written by a Mrs. Fleetwood Habergam, *circa* 1689, who, "undone by the extravagance, and disgraced by the vices of her husband," soothed her sorrows by writing of her woes in the symbolism of flowers. But this, of course, is merely a case of "intrusion."

Chappell (*Popular Music of the Olden Time*), who suggests that Mrs. Habergam's lines were originally sung to the tune of "Come open the door, sweet Betty," prints a traditional tune noted down by Sir George Macfarren.

For other tunes set to the same or similar words, see the *Journal of the Folk-Song Society*, *Songs of the West*, *Traditional Tunes* (Kidson), *English County Songs*, *Ancient Irish Music*, etc.

The tune printed in the text, with its octave in the penultimate phrase, is an example of a certain type of English folk-air.

No. 34. *The Sprig of Thyme*

ALTHOUGH this and the preceding song probably spring from the same root, it is, I think, quite possible to distinguish them, both tunes and words. "The Sprig of Thyme" is, I imagine, the older of the two. Its tone is usually modal, very sad and intense, and somewhat rugged and forceful in character; while its words are abstract and reflective, and sometimes obscure. On the other hand, the words of "The Seeds of Love," although symbolical, are quite clear in their meaning; they are more modern in their diction, and are usually sung to a bright, flowing melody, generally in the major mode.

For other versions with words, see the *Journal of the Folk-Song Society* (volume ii, p. 288); *Folk Songs from Dorset* (p. 10); and *Songs of the West* (No. 7, 2d ed.).

The words in the text are those that the singer sang me, supplemented from those of other sets in my collection. I used the tune, which is in the Æolian mode, for the "Still music" in Mr. Granville Barker's production of *A Midsummer Night's Dream* (Act iv, Sc. 1).

No. 35. *The Cuckoo*

FOR other versions with tunes, see *Folk Songs from Dorset* (No. 11); *Butterworth's Folk Songs from Sussex* (No. 6); *A Garland of Country Song* (No. 1); and Barrett's *English Folk Song* (No. 42).

I have taken down fifteen different versions of this song, but the tune given in the text is the only one that is modal (Æolian). This particular tune is usually associated with the words of "High Germany." Halliwell, in his *Nursery Rhymes* (p. 99), prints a couple of verses in dialect, as follows:

> *The cuckoo's a vine bird,*
> *A zengs as a vlies;*
> *A brengs us good tidin's,*
> *And tells us no lies.*

A zucks th' smael birds' eggs,
To make his voice clear;
And the mwore a cries " cuckoo!"
The zummer draws near.

The words in the text are similar to those given in a Glasgow Garland, "The Sailor's Return."

No. 36. *Blackbirds and Thrushes*
ALTHOUGH I have collected five variants of this song, I do not know of any published version of it. I have had to amend some of the lines that were corrupt.

No. 37. *The Drownea Lover*
FOR other versions with tunes, see *Traditional Tunes* (p. 112); *Journal of the Folk-Song Society* (volume iii, p. 258); and *Songs of the West* (No. 32, 2d ed.). In a note to the latter, Mr. Baring-Gould states that the earliest copy of the words is in the *Roxburghe Ballads*, under the heading "Captain Digby's Farewell;" and that the song afterward came to be applied—at any rate, in the West of England—to the death of the Earl of Sandwich after the action in Sole Bay in 1673. Mr. Baring-Gould suggests that "Stokes Bay," in the version given in the text, is a corruption of "Sole Bay." In both the other versions above cited, and in another one which I have published (*Folk Songs from Various Counties*, No. 8), the scene is laid in the North of England, the lovers being buried in Robin Hood's Churchyard.

The air is in the Dorian mode. The words are almost exactly as they were sung to me.

No. 38. *The Sign of the Bonny Blue Bell*
THE subject of the ballad is clearly related to "I'm going to be married on Sunday," in Dr. Joyce's *Ancient Irish Music* (No. 17); while the first three lines of the initial stanza are identical with the corresponding lines of another song in the same volume (No. 72). The words are printed on a broadside by Williamson, Newcastle (*circa* 1850), and two short verses are given by Halliwell in his *Nursery Rhymes* (p. 94).

A country-dance air, which, however, has nothing in common with the tune in the text, is printed by Walsh (1708), and in *The Dancing Master* (volume ii, ed. 1719), under the heading "I mun be marry'd a Tuesday."

The tune in the text is in the Æolian mode.

No. 39. *O Waly, Waly*
I HAVE collected five variants of this song. The words are so closely allied to the well-known Scottish ballad, "Waly, Waly, up the bank" (*Orpheus Caledonius*), that I have published them under the same title. A close variant is to be found in *Songs of the West* (No. 86, 2d ed.) under the heading "A Ship came Sailing." Mr. Baring-Gould, in a note to the latter, points out that the third stanza is in "The Distressed Virgin," a ballad by Martin Parker, printed by J. Coles, 1646–74.

The traditional "Waly, Waly" is part of a long ballad, "Lord Jamie Douglas," printed in the appendix to Motherwell's *Minstrelsy*. Its origin seems very obscure. The tune is given in Rimbault's *Musical Illustrations of Percy's Reliques* (p. 102); in Chambers's *Scottish Songs prior to Burns* (p. 280); and elsewhere.

No. 40. *Green Bushes*
OTHER versions with tunes may be seen in the *Journal of the Folk-Song Society* (volume v, p. 177); *Songs of the West* (No. 43, 2d ed.); *English County Songs* (p. 170); and *Traditional Tunes* (p. 47). Two stanzas of this song were sung in Buckstone's play, "The Green Bushes" (1845), and, owing to the popularity which this achieved, the complete song was shortly afterward published as a "popular Irish ballad sung by Mrs. FitzWilliam." There are several Irish variants of this tune in the *Petrie Collection* (Nos. 222, 223, 368, 603, etc.), but none of these are downright Mixolydian tunes like the one in the text, which is the form in which the air is usually sung in England. Miss Broadwood and Miss Gilchrist, in notes appended to the version published in the *Journal of the Folk-Song Society*, consider that the words have been affected by those of a "Dialogue in imitation of Mr. H. Purcell—Between a Town

Spark and a Country Lass," 1740. It is difficult to say whether this be so or not, but I think that the phraseology of some of the lines in the text—which are also on broadsides by Disley and Such—shows distinct signs of "editing." Mr. Baring-Gould pronounces the words as "substantially old," "the softening down of an earlier ballad which has its analogue in Scotland," and I suspect that this is the true explanation.

No. 41. *Bedlam*

For other versions with words, see the *Journal of the Folk-Song Society* (volume i, p. 146; volume ii, pp. 37, 93, and 292; volume iii, pp. 111 and 290); *English County Songs* (p. 71); and *Songs of the West* (No. 92).

For words only, see Garret's *Newcastle Garlands* (volumes i and ii), and Logan's *A Pedlar's Pack of Ballads and Songs* (pp. 172-189)

"Mad songs" are great favorites with English folksingers, and I have collected several examples. The tune in the text is frankly a harmonic melody, chiefly remarkable for its very beautiful final phrase.

No. 42. *The Bold Fisherman*

For other versions with tunes, see the *Journal of the Folk-Song Society* (volume i, p.138; volume v, pp. 132-135); and *English County Songs* (p.110).

I have always felt that there was something mystical about this song, and I was accordingly much interested to find that the same idea had independently occurred to Miss Lucy Broadwood, who, in the *Journal of the Folk-Song Society* (volume v, pp. 132, 133), has developed her theory in a very interesting manner. She believes that the "Bold Fisherman," as it appears on broadsides, is but "a vulgar and secularized transmutation of a mediæval allegorical legend," and points out that the familiar elements of Gnostic and Early Christian mystical literature, for example, "the River, the Sea, the royal Fisher, the three Vestures of Light (or Robes of Glory), the Recognition and Adoration by the illuminated humble Soul, the free Pardon," etc., are all to be found among variants of this ballad. The early

Fathers of the Christian Church wrote of their baptized members as "fish," emerged from the waters of baptism. For a full exposition of this view, however, the reader is referred to the note above mentioned.

I have several variants, and I think in every case the tune is in 5-time. The words in the text have been compiled from the sets given me by various singers.

No. 43. *The Rambling Sailor*

For other versions with tunes, see the *Journal of the Folk-Song Society* (volume iii, p. 108; volume v, p. 61); and *Songs of the West* (No. 87, 2d ed.). The tune, like the one in the text, is nearly always in the Mixolydian mode, and usually in hornpipe rhythm. The words on the older broadsides were always about a soldier, not a sailor, but on more modern stall copies, the latter is given the preference. The singer could remember only the first two verses; the third has been "lifted" from the broadside.

No. 44. *Dabbling in the Dew*

This is a very popular song all over England, and I have taken down a large number of variants. The words, which vary but little, are very free and unconventional. I have therefore taken some of the lines in the text from Halliwell's *Nursery Rhymes* (p. 35). In some versions, it is "strawberry leaves," not "dabbling in the dew," that "makes the milkmaids fair"—which I am told, though I have not been able to verify it, is the version given in *Mother Goose's Melodies for Children* (Boston, ed. 1719).

The tune is in the Æolian mode.

For other versions with words, see the *Journal of the Folk-Song Society* (volume iv, pp. 282-285); *Songs of the Four Nations* (p. 58); *English Folk Songs for Schools* (No. 23); and Butterworth's *Folk Songs from Sussex* (No. 9).

No. 45. *The Saucy Sailor*

Other versions with tunes are published in the *Journal of the Folk-Song Society* (volume v, pp. 343-345); Tozer's *Sailors' Songs* (No. 39); Barrett's *English Folk Songs* (No. 32); *Songs of the West* (No. 21); and *English Folk Songs for Schools* (No. 37).

Dr. Barrett, in a footnote, says that the song was a great favorite with factory girls in the East End of London, where, I am told, it is still to be heard.

That printed in *English Folk Songs for Schools* is undoubtedly the normal form of the tune, which is always in the major, or Mixolydian, mode. The mode in which the air given in the text is cast is the Æolian with a sharpened third, the only instance of this irregular scale that I have ever come across—probably the unconscious invention of the singer who gave me the song. The tune is a variant of the air traditionally associated with "Chevy Chase" (see *Northumbrian Minstrelsy*, p. 3, and *Traditional Tunes*, p. 19). Chappell mates the tune to "The Children in the Wood," but states that it was known to be one of the "Chevy Chase" airs.

No. 46. *Fanny Blair*

THE words that I took down from the singer of this song were very corrupt and almost unintelligible. I have therefore substituted lines taken from a Catnach broadside in my possession.

The tune is a very curious one. The singer varied both the seventh and third notes of the scale, sometimes singing them major and sometimes minor in a most capricious manner, so that I can only give the tune in the form in which he most frequently sang it. In *English Folk Song: Some Conclusions* (pp. 71, 72), I have expressed the opinion that in my experience English folksingers very rarely vary the notes of the mode, except, of course, in Mixolydian-Dorian tunes. Mr. Percy Grainger's researches in Lincolnshire, however (*Journal of the Folk-Song Society*, volume iii, pp. 147-242), appear to show that this feeling for the pure diatonic scale is not shared by the folksingers of that county.

No. 47. *Arise, arise*

I HAVE taken down four variants of this ballad, but I do not know of any published form of it.

The tune is partly Mixolydian. The words have not been altered, although I have made use of all the sets that I have collected.

No. 48. *Searching for Lambs*

So far as I know, this has not been published elsewhere. The tune is modal, but lacking the sixth of the scale, it may be either Æolian or Dorian—I have harmonized it in the latter mode. The words are almost exactly as they were sung to me. Taking words and tune together, I consider this to be a very perfect example of a folksong.

No. 49. *Green Broom*

FOR other versions with words, see *Pills to Purge Melancholy* (volume vi, p. 100, ed. 1720); *Songs of the West* (No. 10); *Northumbrian Minstrelsy* (p. 98); and *English County Songs* (p. 88). The words are on broadsides by Such, Pratt, and others, and also in *Gammer Gurton's Garland*.

No. 50. *The Bonny Lighter-Boy*

I HAVE not heard any one sing this song except the man who gave me this version. Nor do I know of any published form of it. The tune is in the Æolian mode. The words in the text, except for four lines in the first verse which the singer could not remember, are as they were sung to me.

No. 51. *The Sweet Primeroses*

THIS is one of the most common of English folksongs. The words are on broadsides by Barraclough of Nuneaton and others. Variants of the tune are given in Barrett's *English Folk Songs* (No. 46), and in the *Journal of the Folk-Song Society* (volume i, p. 21). In the version of the tune given here the rhythm is quite regular, differing in that particular from all other forms of the air that I know. Barrett, in a footnote, states: "This song is usually sung without any attempt to emphasize the rhythm."

The words have been compiled from those supplied to me by several singers.

No. 52. *My Bonny, Bonny Boy*

THE earliest form of the ballad is, perhaps, that which was printed in the reign of Charles II under several titles, "Cupid's Trappan," "The Twitcher," "Bonny, bonny Bird," etc. (Chappell's *Popular Music of the Olden Time*, p. 555). For other versions with tunes, see the *Journal of the Folk-Song Society* (volume i, pp. 17 and 274; volume ii, p. 82; volume iii, p. 85); *Songs of the West* (No. 106, 2d ed.); *English County Songs* (p. 146); *Folk Songs from Various Counties* (No. 9). The words are also in the *Roxburghe Collection* and printed in black-letter by J. Coles and by W. Thackeray (17th century). Mr. Baring-Gould claims that "bird," not "boy," is the proper reading, and points out that it is so given in the oldest printed version. But Miss Broadwood suggests that an old ballad-title "My bonny *Burd*" (or young girl) may have led to the allegorical use of the bird in later forms of the ballad.

The version given in the text was recovered in London. It was necessary to make one or two slight alterations in the words. The tune, which is in the Æolian mode, contains a passage only rarely heard in folksong, in which several notes are sung to a single syllable (see *English Folk Song: Some Conclusions*, p. 109).

No. 53 a and b. *As I walked through the meadows*

FOR other versions, see the *Journal of the Folk-Song Society* (volume ii, pp. 10-12; volume v, p. 94). A few verbal alterations have been made in the words. The first tune is in the major mode and the second in the Mixolydian with, in one passage, a sharpened seventh.

No. 54. *Erin's Lovely Home*

OTHER versions with tunes are printed in the *Journal of the Folk-Song Society* (volume i, p. 117; volume ii, pp. 167 and 211); and the *Journal of the Irish Folk-Song Society* (Part I, p. 11).

The words are on broadsides by Such and others.

The tune is almost invariably a modal one, either Æolian or, as in the present case, Dorian.

No. 55. *The True Lover's Farewell*

FOR other versions with tunes of this ballad and of "The Turtle Dove," with which it is closely allied, see the *Journal of the Folk-Song Society* (volume ii, p. 55; volume iii, p. 86; volume iv, p. 286).

The song is clearly one of several peasant songs of the same type upon which Burns modelled his "A red, red rose" (see note to the song in *The Centenary Burns* by Henley and Henderson). The old Scottish tune is printed in Johnson's *Museum* under the heading "Queen Mary's Lament." The variants of this very beautiful song that have been recently recovered in the southern counties of England prove beyond doubt that this was the source from which Burns borrowed nearly all his lines. Henderson, indeed, states that a broadside containing one of the versions of this song was known to have been in Burns's possession. Two of the traditional stanzas are included in an American burlesque song, dating from about the middle of the last century, called "My Mary Anne" (see the *Journal of the Folk-Song Society*, volume iii, p. 89; volume iv, p. 288). Three stanzas in the text are similar to corresponding lines in a garland entitled "The true Lover's Farewell," the second of "Five excellent New Songs, printed in the year 1792." The words have been compiled from several traditional sets that I have collected.

The tune is in the Dorian mode.

No. 56. *High Germany*

THERE are two ballads of this name. The words of one of them, that given here, may be found on a broadside by Such and in *A Collection of Choice Garlands*, *circa* 1780. The second is printed on a Catnach broadside, and is entitled "The True Lovers: or the King's command must be obeyed," although it is popularly known as "High Germany." For versions of both of these, see the *Journal of the Folk-Song Society* (volume ii, p. 25); *Journal of the Irish Folk-Song Society* (Part I, p. 10); and *Folk Songs from Dorset* (No. 6).

The words have been compiled from different versions. The tune is in the Æolian mode.

No. 57. *Sweet Lovely Joan*

THE only variant of this that I know of is printed in the *Journal of the Folk-Song Society* (volume i, p. 270) and harmonized by Dr. R. Vaughan Williams in *Folk Songs from Sussex* (No. 14). As the singer could give me but five stanzas, I have had to complete his song from a broadside in my possession (no imprint). The tune, which is remarkable for the irregularity of its rhythm, is in the Æolian mode.

No. 58. *My Boy Willie*

A YORKSHIRE version of the words is given by Halliwell in his *Popular Rhymes* (p. 328); and a Scottish variant in Herd's *Scottish Songs* (volume ii, p. 1). See also Baring-Gould's *A Book of Nursery Songs and Rhymes* (No. 24).

The song, I imagine, is a comic derivative, or burlesque, of "Lord Rendal."

No. 59. *Whistle, Daughter, Whistle*

I HAVE taken down two variants of this song, and Joyce prints an Irish version under the heading "Cheer up, cheer up, Daughter," in his *Ancient Irish Music* (No. 26).

The words given me by the singer were a little too free and unconventional to be published without emendation, but the necessary alterations have, nevertheless, been very few and unimportant. The tune is in the Æolian mode.

No. 60. *Mowing the Barley*

FOR other versions, see *Wiltshire Folk Songs and Carols* (Rev. G. Hill); Butterworth's *Folk Songs from Sussex* (No. 4); and *Folk Songs from Various Counties* (No. 4).

No. 61. *I'm Seventeen come Sunday*

THIS ballad, with words re-written by Burns, is in *The Scots Musical Museum* (ed. 1792, No. 397). The tune there given, which is different from ours, is a traditional one, and was recorded by Burns himself from a singer in Nithsdale. Other versions are printed in the *Journal of the Folk-Song Society* (volume i, p. 92; volume ii, pp. 9 and 269); *Songs of the West* (No. 73, 2d ed.); and Ford's *Vagabond Songs and Ballads* (p. 99).

The words, which are on broadsides by Bebbington (Manchester) and Such, have not been altered. The tune is in the Dorian mode.

No. 62. *The Lark in the Morn*

FOR other versions with tunes, see *Folk Songs from the Eastern Counties* (No. 6); *A Garland of Country Song* (No. 27); *Traditional Tunes* (p. 145); and the *Journal of the Folk-Song Society* (volume ii, p. 272).

No. 63. *Hares on the Mountains*

THIS is a very popular song in the West of England, but it has not, I believe, been found elsewhere. Similar words are in Sam Lover's *Rory O'More* (p. 101), which Mr. Hermann Löhr has set to music. There is also a tune in the *Petrie Collection* (No. 821), called "If all the young maidens be blackbirds and thrushes," in the same metre as the lines in *Rory O'More*. Probably the song is of folk-origin and was known to Sam Lover, who placed it in the mouth of one of the characters in his novel, adding himself, presumably, the last stanza.

No. 64. *O Sally, my dear*

THIS, of course, is clearly allied to the preceding song. I have collected only two other versions of it. The words of the first three stanzas had, of necessity, to be somewhat altered. The tune is in the Æolian mode.

No. 65. *Gently, Johnny, my Jingalo*

I HAVE taken down only one other variant of this. The words were rather coarse, but I have, I think, managed to re-write the first and third lines of each verse without sacrificing the character of the original song. The singer told me he learned it from his father. I have no doubt but that it is a genuine folksong. The tune is partly Mixolydian.

No. 66. *The Keys of Canterbury*

FOR other versions with tunes, see the *Journal of the Folk-Song Society* (volume ii, p. 85); *English County Songs* (p. 32); *Songs of the West* (No. 22,

2d ed.); and Mason's *Nursery Rhymes and Country Songs* (p. 67). Halliwell (*Nursery Rhymes and Tales*, p. 96) quotes a version of the words. The same theme is dramatized in the Singing Game, "There stands a Lady" (*Children's Singing Games*, Set 3, Novello & Co.).

The tune, which is in the Æolian mode, is remarkable in that it is practically constructed upon the first five notes of the scale—the sixth is but once used, and then only as an auxiliary note.

No. 67. *My Man John*

THIS is obviously but an extension of the preceding song in which a third character is introduced. I have taken down four other versions, one of which is printed in the *Journal of the Folk-Song Society* (volume ii, p. 88). Mr. Baring-Gould gives the words of yet another variant in his note to "Blue Muslin" (*Songs of the West*, p. 8, 2d ed.), where he also points out that muslin was introduced into England in 1670, and that mous-e-line is the old form of the word.

No. 68. *O No, John!*

I HAVE collected several versions of this song. The first stanza is identical with the initial verse of the Singing Game, "Lady on the Mountain" (*Dictionary of British Folk-Lore*, volume i, pp. 320-324). Lady Gomme shrewdly guesses that the game was derived from a ballad, and Mr. Newell, in his *Games and Songs of American Children* (p. 55), prints a version which he also believes to be "an old English song, which has been taken for a ring-game." See also "The Disdainful Lady," in Miss Burne's *Shropshire Folk-Lore* (p. 561); and "Twenty, Eighteen," in *English County Songs* (p. 90).

The main theme of the song—the daughter's promise to her father to answer "No" to all her suitors during his absence—is not in any of the songs above mentioned. The idea, however, is carried out in "No, Sir!" which the late Miss A. M. Wakefield made very popular some years ago. Miss Wakefield wrote to me: "I first heard something like it from an American governess.

Neither words nor music were at all complete. . . . I wrote it down and it got a good deal altered and I never looked upon it at all as a folksong," and added that her song was now sung by the Salvation Army, under the title "Yes, Lord!" The song is, of course, closely allied to the two preceding songs. The tune is a variant of the "Billy Taylor" tune (see No. 71). The Shropshire version and the one in *English County Songs* are Dorian and Æolian (?) variants of the same air. The first two stanzas of the text are exactly as they were sung to me; the rest of the lines were coarse and needed considerable revision.

No. 69. *The Brisk Young Bachelor*

THE troubles of married life, from either the husband's or the wife's point of view, form the subject of many folksongs. One of the best and oldest examples is "A woman's work is never done," reproduced in Ashton's *Century of Ballads* (p. 26). I have collected several songs that harp on the same theme, two of which are printed respectively in the *Journal of the Folk-Song Society* (volume v, p. 65), and *Folk-Songs from Various Counties* (No. 10).

The tune, which is in the Dorian mode, is a fine example of the rollicking folk-air. As the singer's words were incomplete, I have supplemented them with lines from my other versions.

No. 70. *Ruggleton's Daughter of Iero*

THIS song, of which I have only collected one variant, is a version of a very ancient ballad, the history of which may be traced in Child's *English and Scottish Ballads* (No. 227), and in Miss Gilchrist's note to "The Wee Cooper of Fife," in the *Journal of the Folk-Song Society* (volume ii, pp. 223, 224). In some versions the husband is deterred from beating his wife through fear of her "gentle kin." To evade this difficulty he kills one of his own wethers, strips off its skin, and lays it on her back, saying:

> *I dare na thump you, for your proud kin,*
> *But well sall I lay to my ain wether's skin.*

(See "Sweet Robin," in Jamieson's *Popular Ballads*, volume i, p. 319.)

This motive is absent from the present version, of which it may or may not once have formed part. For it is possible to argue that the "wether's skin" motive is an addition, which became attached to an older and simpler form of the ballad. The facts, as they stand, admit of either interpretation.

There is yet a third variation of the story in "Robin-a-thrush (see *English County Songs*, *The Besom Maker*, *English Folk Songs for Schools*, etc.), in which the story is still further curtailed by the omission of the wife-beating episode. In this latter form, it becomes a nursery nonsense-song, which relates in humorous fashion the ridiculous muddles made by a slovenly and incompetent wife. Its connection with "Ruggleton" or "Sweet Robin" is to be inferred from the title and refrain, "Robin-a-thrush," which, as Miss Gilchrist has pointed out, is probably a corruption of "Robin he thrashes her."

I have collected another song which has some affinity with "Ruggleton." Here the husband married his wife on Monday; cut "a twig of holly so green" on Tuesday; "hung it out to dry" on Wednesday; on Thursday he "beat her all over the shoulders and head, till he had a-broke his holly green twig;" on Friday she "opened her mouth and began to roar;" and, finally,

> *On Saturday morning I breakfast without*
> *A scolding wife or a brawling bout.*
> *Now I can enjoy my bottle and friend;*
> *I think I have made a rare week's end.*

The same motive is to be found in "The Husband's Complaint," printed in Herd's *Manuscripts*, edited by Dr. Hans Hecht (p. 106).

The words given in the text are almost exactly as they were sung to me. I have, however, transposed the order of the words "brew" and "bake" in the fourth and fifth verses, in order to restore some semblance of a rhyme. Clearly there was some corruption; but whether my emendation is the correct one or not, it is difficult to say. There is a fragment, quoted by Jamieson, in which the verse in question is rendered:

> *She wadna bake, she wadna brew,*
> (Hollin, green hollin),
> *For spoiling o' her comely hue,*
> (Bend your bow, Robin).

There is, too, a version in *The Journal of American Folk-Lore* (volume vii, p. 253), quoted by Child, which is closely allied to the song in the text. In this variant, the following stanza occurs:

> *Jenny couldn't wash and Jenny couldn't bake,*
> Gently Jenny cried rosemaree,
> *For fear of dirting her white apurn tape,*
> As the dew flies over the mulberry tree.

No. 71. *William Taylor*

FOR other versions with tunes, see the *Journal of the Folk-Song Society* (volume i, p. 254; volume iii, pp. 214–220); and *Folk Songs from Somerset* (No. 118). No tune is better known to the average English folksinger than this. It is usually in the major or, as in the present case, in the Mixolydian mode, but occasionally (see the versions cited above) in the Dorian or Æolian. A burlesque version of the words, with an illustration by George Cruikshank, is given in the *Universal Songster* (volume i, p. 6). "Billy Taylor" became a very popular street-song during the first half of the last century, and I suspect that it was during that period that the last stanza in the text was added.

No. 72. *Sweet William*

OTHER versions are given in the *Journal of the Folk-Song Society* (volume i, p. 99); *English County Songs* (p. 74); and Christie's *Traditional Ballad Airs* (volume i, p. 248). The song is a very common one and I have noted several variants of it.

No. 73. *The Watchet Sailor*

I HAVE only one variant of this song, "Threepenny Street," and so far as I know it has not been published elsewhere. Compare the tune, which is in the Æolian mode, with that of "Henry Martin" in this collection (No. 1).

No. 74. *Scarborough Fair*

FOR other versions, see *Songs of the West* (No. 48, 2d ed.); *English County Songs* (p. 12); *Traditional*

Tunes (pp. 42 and 172); *Northumbrian Minstrelsy* (p. 79); *Folk Songs from Somerset* (No. 64); *Journal of the Folk-Song Society* (volume i, p. 83; volume ii, p. 212; volume iii, p. 274), etc.

This is one of the ancient Riddle Songs, a good example of which occurs in the Wanderer scene in the first act of Wagner's *Siegfried*. In its usual form, one person imposes a task upon his adversary, who, however, evades it by setting another task of equal difficulty, which, according to the rules of the game, must be performed first. In the version given here, the replies are omitted. For an exhaustive exposition of the subject, see Child's "Elfin Knight," and "Riddles wisely expounded," in his *English and Scottish Popular Ballads*. See, also, Kinloch's *Ancient Scottish Ballads* (p. 145); Motherwell's *Minstrelsy* (Appendix, p. 1); Buchan's *Ancient Ballads of the North of Scotland* (volume ii, p. 296); *Gesta Romanorum* (pp. xl, 124, and 233, Bohn ed.); *Gammer Gurton's Garland*; and Halliwell's *Nursery Rhymes*. Mr. Baring-Gould's note to the song in *Songs of the West* should also be consulted.

The tune is in the Dorian mode, except for the final and very unusual cadence. The words have been supplemented from those of other traditional versions which I have collected.

No. 75. *Brimbledon Fair*, or *Young Ramble-Away*

MR. KIDSON prints a major version of this song in his *Traditional Tunes* (p. 150), under the heading "Brocklesby Fair." The words are on a broadside, "Young Ramble Away," by Jackson of Birmingham. The tune is in the Dorian mode.

No. 76. *Bridgwater Fair*

ST. MATTHEW'S FAIR at Bridgwater is a very ancient one, and is still a local event of some importance, although it has seen its best days. The tune, which is partly Mixolydian, is a variant of "Gently, Johnny, my Jingalo" (No. 65), and also of "Bibberly Town" (*Songs of the West*, No. 110, 2d ed.). I have only one other variant of this, from which, however, some of the lines in the text have been taken.

No. 77. *The Crabfish*

A SCOTTISH version of this curious song, "The Crab," is given in *A Ballad Book* by C. K. Sharpe and Edmund Goldsmid (volume ii, p. 10), published in 1824. The footnote states that the song is founded upon a story in *Le Moyen de Parvenir*. Some of the words have been altered.

The tune is in the Mixolydian mode, and was sung to me very excitedly and at break-neck speed, the singer punctuating the rhythm of the refrain with blows of her fist upon the table at which she was sitting.

No. 78. *The Beggar*

THE words of the refrain of this song are very nearly identical with the chorus of "I cannot eat but little meat," the well-known drinking-song in *Gammer Gurton's Needle*. This play was printed in 1575 and, until the discovery of *Royster Doyster*, was considered to be the earliest English comedy. Its author was John Still, afterwards, that is, 1592, Bishop of Bath and Wells. The song, however, was not written by him, for Chappell points out that "the Rev. Alex. Dyce has given a copy of double length from a manuscript in his possession and certainly of an earlier date than the play." Chappell furthermore calls attention to the custom of singing old songs or playing old tunes at the commencement, and at the end, of the acts of early dramas. "I cannot eat" has been called "the first drinking-song of any merit in our language."

The words of this Exmoor song, excluding the chorus, are quite different from the version in *Gammer Gurton's Needle*. It appears that under the title of "The Beggar and the Queen," they were published in the form of a song not more than a century ago (see *A Collection of English Ballads from beginning of Eighteenth Century*, volume vii, Brit. Mus.). The tune, which is quite different from the one given here, is clearly the invention of a contemporary composer, but there is no evidence to show whether or not the words were the production of a contemporary writer; they may have been traditional verses which happened to attract the attention of some musician.

There is a certain air of reckless abandonment about them which seems to suggest a folk-origin, and they are, at any rate, far less obviously the work of a literary man than are the verses—apart from the refrain—of "I cannot eat."

In *The Songster's Museum* (Gosport), there is a parody of the above song (chorus omitted), which, in the *Bagford Ballads* (volume i, p. 214), are attributed to Tom Dibdin.

A tune to "I cannot eat" is given in Ritson, and in *Popular Music of the Olden Time* (p. 72), and is a version of "John Dory." The tune in the text has no relation whatever to that well-known air, nor to any other tune that I know of. In my opinion, it may well be a genuine folk-air.

The singer gave me two verses only, the second and third in the text. The other two are from a version which the Rev. S. Baring-Gould collected in Devon, and which he has courteously allowed me to use. Mr. H. E. D. Hammond has recovered similar words in Dorset, but, like Mr. Baring-Gould, he found them mated to quite a modern and "composed" air.

No. 79. *The Keeper*

THIS is one of the few two-men folksongs. I have several variants of it, but the words of all of them, except this particular one, were so corrupt as to be unintelligible. The words are printed in an old garland, from which the last stanza in the text has been derived. The rest of the words are given as they were sung to me.

No. 80. *The Three Sons*

FOR other versions with tunes, see *English County Songs* (p. 20), and Miss Mason's *Nursery Rhymes and Country Songs* (p. 7).

No. 81. *Jack Hall*

JACK HALL, who had been sold to a chimney-sweep for a guinea, was executed for burglary at Tyburn in 1701. The song must have been written before 1719, for in *Pills to Purge Melancholy* (volume ii, p. 182), there is a song, "The Moderator's Dream," "the words made to a pretty tune, call'd Chimney Sweep," which is in iden-

tically the same metre as that of "Jack Hall." A vulgarized edition of the song was made very popular in the middle years of the last century by a comic singer, G. W. Ross.

I have taken down four versions, the tunes of which, with the exception of that given in the text, are all variants of the "Admiral Benbow" air (see No. 87). The metre in which each of these two ballads is cast is so unusual that we may assume that one was written in imitation of the other. As Jack Hall was executed in 1701 and Admiral Benbow was killed in 1702, it is probable that "Jack Hall" is the earlier of the two.

The singer could recall the words of one verse only. The remaining stanzas have been taken from my other versions. The tune is in the Æolian mode.

No. 82. *Driving away at the Smoothing Iron*

I HAVE noted two other versions of this song. The tune is a variant of "All round my hat," a popular song of the early years of the last century. Chappell, in his *Ancient English Melodies* (No. 126), prints a version of the air and dubs it "a Somersetshire tune, the original of 'All round my hat.'" I believe it to be a genuine folk-air, which, as in other cases, formed the basis of a street-song.

No. 83. *The Robber*

THE words to which this remarkably fine Dorian air was sung were about a highwayman and his sweetheart, but were too fragmentary for publication. I have wedded the tune to a different, but similar, set of words which another singer sang to a very poor tune.

No. 84. *John Barleycorn*

FOR other versions with tunes of this well-known ballad, see *Songs of the West* (No. 14 and Note, 2d ed.); Barrett's *English Folk Songs* (No. 8); *Journal of the Folk-Song Society* (volume i, p. 81; volume iii, p. 255); and Christie's *Traditional Ballad Airs of Scotland* (volume i, p. 134).

The earliest printed copy of the ballad is of the time of James I.

Versions with words only are given in Dick's *Songs of Robert Burns* (p. 314); *Roxburghe Ballads* (volume ii, p. 327); and Bell's *Ballads and Songs of the Peasantry of England* (p. 80). Chappell gives "Stingo or Oil of Barley" as the traditional air; while Dick says it is uncertain whether Burns intended his version of the ballad to be sung to that tune or to "Lull me beyond thee."

It is not easy to express in musical notation the exact way in which the singer sang this song. He dwelt, perhaps, rather longer upon the double-dotted notes than their written value, although not long enough to warrant their being marked with the formal pause. The singer told me that he heard the song solemnly chanted by some street-singers who passed through his village when he was a child. The song fascinated him and he followed the singers and tried to learn the air. For some time afterward he was unable to recall it, when one day, to his great delight, the tune suddenly came back to him, and since then he has constantly sung it. He gave me the words of the first stanza only. The remaining verses in the text have been taken from Bell's *Songs of the Peasantry of England*. The tune, which is in the Æolian mode, is such a fine one that I have been tempted to harmonize it somewhat elaborately. Those who prefer a simpler setting can repeat the harmonies set to the first verse.

No. 85. *Poor Old Horse*

FOR other versions with tunes, see the *Journal of the Folk-Song Society* (volume i, pp. 75 and 260; volume ii, p. 263); Miss Mason's *Nursery Rhymes and Country Songs* (p. 49); *Songs of the West* (No. 77, 2d ed.); and *Songs of Northern England* (p. 60).

The song was evidently one that was sung during the ceremony of the hobby horse, for example, the Hooden Horse in Kent (see *The Hooden Horse*, by Percy Maylam). A kindred ceremony, also associated with a song, "The Dead Horse," is still celebrated by sailors after they have been a month at sea (*English Folk Chanteys*, p. 73).

The tune is partly Mixolydian.

No. 86. *Botany Bay*

I DO not know of any published versions of this song. I made use of the tune in Mr. Granville Barker's production of Hardy's *Dynasts*, setting the words of the "Trafalgar" song to it.

No. 87. *Admiral Benbow*

CHAPPELL (*Popular Music of the Olden Time*, volume ii, pp. 642 and 678) gives two versions of this ballad. The first of these is entirely different from that given in the text; but the words of the second version, which are taken from Halliwell's *Early Naval Ballads of England*, are substantially the same, though set to a different air. The air "Marrinys yn Tiger," in Mr. Gill's *Manx National Songs* (p. 4), is a variant of our tune. Messrs. Kidson and Moffat publish a variant of the first of Chappell's versions in *Minstrelsy of England* (p. 25) with an instructive note. See also Ashton's *Real Sailor Songs* (p. 19).

John Benbow (1653–1702) was the son of a tanner at Shrewsbury. He was apprenticed to a butcher, from whose shop he ran away to sea. He entered the navy and rose rapidly to high command. The ballad is concerned with his engagement with the French fleet, under Du Casse, off the West Indies, August 19–24, 1702. The English force consisted of seven ships, of from fifty to seventy guns. Benbow's ship was the *Breda*. Captain Walton of the *Ruby* was the only one of his captains to stand by him; the rest shirked. The *Ruby* was disabled on August 23, and left for Port Royal. Shortly afterwards Benbow's right leg was shattered by a chain shot. After his wound was dressed, he insisted on being carried up to the quarter-deck, as narrated in the ballad. On the following day, his captains, headed by Captain Kirkby of the *Defiance*, came on board and urged him to discontinue the chase. This they compelled him to do, and he returned to Jamaica, where he at once ordered a court-martial. Captains Kirkby and Wade were sentenced to be shot; Vincent and Fogg were suspended; while Captain Hudson of the *Pendennis* died before the trial. Kirkby and Wade were executed on board the *Bristol*, in Plymouth Sound, on

April 16, 1703. Admiral Benbow succumbed to his wounds November 4, 1702, at Port Royal, and was buried at Kingston. His portrait is, or was, in the Painted Hall, Greenwich, to which it was presented by George IV. Mr. Ashton states that there is a tradition "that his body was brought to England and buried in Deptford Church."

It is a little difficult to account for the popularity Benbow excited. Personally brave he certainly was; but he has been described as "an honest rough seaman," who, it is alleged, treated his inferiors with scant courtesy. Their failure to stand by him in the French fight was, of course, a disgraceful act of cowardice; but it may also be attributed, to some extent, to their want of personal regard for their chief.

No. 88. *Bold Nelson's Praise*
THIS is the only version of this song that I know. The singer mixed his words in all the verses except the first one, necessitating a certain amount of rearrangement. The air is in the Dorian mode, and is a variant of "Princess Royal," a well-known Morris-Jig tune. Shield adapted the air to the words of "The Saucy Arethusa," one of the songs in the ballad-opera *The Lock and Key* (1796). The composition of the air has sometimes been attributed to Carolan. The tune is also printed in Walsh's *Compleat Dancing Master* (*circa* 1730), under the title "The Princess Royal: the new way."

No. 89. *Spanish Ladies*
THIS is a Capstan Chantey. It is also well known in the navy, where it is sung as a song, chanteys not being permitted. Captain Kettlewell, R.N., who has made a special study of this song and has very kindly revised the words for me, tells me that when it is sung on board ship, the conclusion of the chorus is, or always used to be, greeted with a shout of "Heave and pawl!" (the pawl is the catch which prevents the recoil of the windlass).

The tune is in the Æolian mode and, in my opinion, it is one of the grandest of our folk-tunes

and one of which a seafaring nation may well be proud. Nowadays, alas! sailors sing a modernized and far less beautiful form of the air in the major mode.

No. 90. *The Ship in Distress*
FOR other versions with tunes, see the *Journal of the Folk-Song Society* (volume iv, pp. 320-323). Ashton, in his *Real Sailor Songs* (No. 44), prints a broadside version of the words. A similar song is sung by French sailors, "Le petit Navire" (Miss Laura A. Smith's *Music of the Waters*, p. 149), of which Thackeray's "Little Billee" was a burlesque.

The tune is in the Dorian mode.

No. 91. *Come all you worthy Christian men*
SEVERAL versions of this moralizing ballad with tunes are printed in the *Journal of the Folk-Song Society* (volume i, p. 74; volume ii, pp. 115-122). The tune is one of the most common, the most characteristic, and, I would add, the most beautiful of English folk-airs. The version here given is in the Æolian mode, but it is often sung in the major, Dorian, and Mixolydian modes. For other versions of the tune set to different words, see *English County Songs* (pp. 34, 68, and 102); and *Songs of the West* (No. 111, 2d ed.). The well-known air "The Miller and the Dee" is a minor and "edited" version of the same tune. Chappell, too, noted down a version of it which he heard sung in the streets of Kilburn in the early years of the last century (*Popular Music*, p. 748). For an exhaustive note by Miss Broadwood upon the tune and its origin, see the *Journal of the Folk-Song Society* (volume ii, p. 119).

No. 92. *Wassail Song*
THE old custom of wassail singing still survives in many parts of England, though it is fast dying out. The ceremony is performed on January 5, *i.e.*, the eve of Epiphany. It is of Saxon origin, the word "wassail" (accent on the last syllable) meaning "be of good health," from A.-S. *wes* = be, and *hāl* = whole or hale. The cup "made of the good old ashen tree" takes us back to the

period when all common domestic vessels were of wood. In early times there was an ecclesiastical edict against the use of wooden vessels for the Holy Communion.

Sir James Ramsay, in his *Foundations of England* (volume ii), quotes an old Saxon "toasting-cry" from Wace, the Anglo-Norman poet (d. 1180). The Chronicler says that the following lines were sung in the English camp on the eve of the battle of Hastings:

> *Bublie crient é weissel,*
> *E laticome é drencheheil*
> *Drinc Hindrewart é Drintome*
> *Drinc Helf, é drinc tome.*

This, according to Sir James Ramsay, may be translated thus:

> *Rejoice and wassail*
> *Let it come (pass the bottle) and drink health*
> *Drink backwards and drink to me*
> *Drink half and drink empty.*

For other versions, see "Somersetshire Wassail" (*A Garland of Country Song*, No. 20); *Sussex Songs* (No. 3); and *The Besom Maker* (p. 9). For a Gloucestershire version, see *English Folk Carols* (No. 21).

The strong tune in the text is in the Dorian mode.

No. 93. *It's a rosebud in June*

THE Rev. John Broadwood noted a Sussex version of this song before 1840 (see *Sussex Songs*, No. 11, Leonard & Company, Oxford Street). The words were also set to music by John Barrett, and were probably sung in "The Custom of the Manor" (1715). As the words of this version show traces of West Country dialect, and the tune, with its Dorian characteristics, is not altogether unlike that printed here, it is just possible that Barrett founded his tune upon the folk-air. The Sussex tune is quite different from our Dorian version, which was collected by me in Somerset. The words are printed exactly as they were sung to me.

No. 94. *A Brisk Young Sailor*

THIS is one of the most popular of English folk-songs. I have collected a large number of variants, from the several sets of which the words in the text have been compiled. For other versions see "There is an ale-house in yonder Town," in the *Journal of the Folk-Song Society* (volume i, p. 252; volume ii, pp. 155, 158, 159, and 168; volume iii, p. 188).

No. 95. *The Sheep-Shearing*

THE tune to which this song is set is, of course, that of "The Sweet Nightingale," a song that is known to almost every folksinger in the West Country (see *Songs of the West*, No. 15, 2d ed.). Bell, in his *Ballads and Songs of the English Peasantry*, prints the words, which he first heard from some Cornish miners at Marienberg and afterwards procured from a gentleman at Plymouth. He erroneously assigns them to the 17th century. For the Rev. S. Baring-Gould has shown that they first appeared in Bickerstaff's "Thomas and Sally" (1760), set to music by Dr. Arne. The West Country tune, however, is quite distinct from Dr. Arne's, and has all the qualities of the genuine folk-air. Mr. Baring-Gould suggests that Bickerstaff's words "travelled down into Cornwall in some such collection as 'The Syren,' and were there set to music by some local genius."

I have collected several variants of "The Sweet Nightingale," and the singer of one of them casually remarked that the tune did not really belong to those words but to a sheep-shearing song. He went on to say that many years ago, when he was a boy, a very old man used to come to his cottage and sing this sheep-shearing song; and then he repeated to me the words of the first stanza, which were all that he could recall. Now the singer was a man of ninety years of age, so that the sheep-shearing song must, presumably, have been in existence before 1760. It will be noticed that in this version of the air, the fourth phrase is not lengthened as it always is when sung to the words of "The Sweet Nightingale." How and why this variation came to be made is an interesting point (see *English Folk Song: Some Conclusions*, p. 110).

No. 96. *The Twelve Days of Christmas*

THIS song consists of twenty-three verses, and is sung in the following way. The second verse begins:

> *On the* eleven *day of Christmas*
> *my true Love sent to me*
> Eleven *bulls a-beating*, etc.,

and so on till the twelfth verse, as given in the text. The process is then reversed, the verses being gradually increased in length, so that the thirteenth verse is:

> *On the* second *day of Christmas*
> *my true Love sent to me*
> Two *turtle doves*
> One *goldie ring*,
> *And the part of a* June *apple-tree.*

In this way the twenty-third verse is triumphantly reached, and that, except for the last line, is the same as the first verse.

Another way to sing the song is to begin with "On the first day of Christmas," etc., and to continue to the "twelfth day," when the song concludes.

"June Apple-Tree" may or may not be a corruption of "Juniper-Tree," but the singer explained it by saying that it meant a tree whose fruit kept sound and good till the following June.

For the third gift, the singer sang "Three Britten Chains," which she said were "sea-birds with golden chains round their necks." All the other singers I have heard sang "Three French Hens," and, as this is the usual reading in printed copies, I have so given it in the text. "Britten Chains" may be a corruption of "Bréton hens."

The "twelve days" are, of course, those between Christmas Day and Epiphany, or Twelfth Day.

For other versions, see Mr. Baring-Gould's note to "The jolly Goss-hawk (*Songs of the West*, No. 71); Chambers's *Popular Songs of Scotland* (p. 42); Halliwell's *Nursery Rhymes* (pp. 63 and 73); and *Northumbrian Minstrelsy* (p. 129), where the song is described as "one of the quaintest of Christmas carols now relegated to the nursery as a forfeit game, where each child in succession has to repeat the gifts of the day and incurs a forfeit for every error." In this last version (also given in Halliwell's *Nursery Rhymes*, p. 73, and Husk's *Songs of the Nativity*), the first gift is "a partridge on a pear tree," and this I have heard several times in country villages. One singer who gave it to me volunteered the statement that it was only another way of singing "part of a Juniper-tree," of which, of course, it may be a corruption.

These words are also used as a Children's Game. One of Halliwell's versions (p. 63) is still used by children in Somerset, and Lady Gomme (*Dictionary of British Folk-Lore*, volume i, p. 315), besides reprinting three of the forms given above, gives a London variant. In a note to the game, Lady Gomme points out that the festival of the twelve days, the great midwinter feast of Yule, was a very important one, and that in this game may, perhaps, be discerned the relic of certain customs and ceremonies and the penalties or forfeits incurred by those who omitted religiously to carry them out; and she adds that it was a very general practice for work of all kinds to be put entirely aside before Christmas and not resumed until after Twelfth Day.

Country singers are very fond of accumulative songs of this type, regarding them as tests of endurance and memory, and sometimes of sobriety!

No. 97. *The Ten Commandments*

THIS song is very common in Somerset and over the whole of the West of England. The Rev. S. Baring-Gould has published a version in *Songs of the West*, and there are two versions in *English County Songs*. Both of these publications contain notes respecting the origin, distribution, and meaning of this curious song.

It will be seen that the words of many of the verses are corrupt; so corrupt, indeed, that in some cases we can do little more than guess at their original meaning. The variants that I have recovered in Somerset are as follows:

(1) All versions agree in this line, which obviously refers to God Almighty.

(2) "Two of these are lizzie both, clothed all in green, O!" Mr. Baring-Gould suggests that

the "lily-white babes" are probably the Gemini, or signs for Spring.

(3) "Thrivers," "Tires," or "Trivers." It has been suggested that these may be corruptions of "Wisers," as one printed version gives it, and may refer to the Wise Men from the East.

(4) Always "Gospel Preachers" or "Makers."

(5) "The boys upon the pole," "The thimble over the ball," "The plum boys at the bowl," or "in the brow."

(6) "Broad Waiters," "Charming Waiters," "Go Waiters," "The Minger Waiters." The editors of *English County Songs* suggest that these may refer to the six water-pots used in the miracle of Cana of Galilee.

(7) Always "Seven stars in the sky"—presumably the constellation of Ursa Major.

(8) "The Gibley Angels," "The Angel Givers," "The Gabriel Angels."

(9) No Somerset variants. Mr. Baring-Gould records a Devon variant, "The Nine Delights," that is, the joys of Mary.

(10) No variants.

(11) "Eleven and eleven is gone to heaven," that is, the twelve Apostles without Judas Iscariot.

(12) No variants.

In *Notes and Queries* for December 26, 1868, there is a version of the words of this song as "sung by the children at Beckington, Somerset." It begins as follows:

> *Sing, sing, what shall we sing?*
> *Sing all over one.*
> *One! What is one?*
> *One they do call the righteous Man.*
> *Save poor souls to rest, Amen.*

These are the remaining verses:

> *Two is the Jewry.*
> *Three is the Trinity.*
> *Four is the open door.*
> *Five is the man alive.*
> *Six is the crucifix.*
> *Seven is the bread of leaven.*
> *Eight is the crooked straight.*
> *Nine is the water wine.*
> *Ten is our Lady's hen.*
> *Eleven is the gate of heaven.*
> *Twelve is the ring of bells.*

A Hebrew version of the words of "The Ten Commandments" is to be found in the service for the Passover (see *Service for the First Nights of Passover according to the custom of the German and Polish Jews*, by the Rev. A. P. Mendes). The service for the second night of the Passover concludes with two recitations, both of which are accumulative songs. The second of these, "One only kid," has nothing to do with "The Ten Commandments," but, as it is analogous to the English nursery song, "The Old Woman and her Pig," it is perhaps worth while to quote the last verse:

> *Then came the Most Holy, blessed be He, and slew the slaughterer, who had slaughtered the ox, which had drunk the water, which had burnt the staff, which had smitten the dog, which had bitten the cat, which had devoured the kid, which my father bought for two zuzim; one only kid, one only kid.*

This, of course, is explained esoterically. The "cat," for instance, refers to Babylon; the "dog" to Persia; the "staff" to Greece, and so on (see Mendes).

The other accumulative song, which precedes "One only kid," is a Hebrew rendering of "The Ten Commandments" of western England. It contains thirteen verses:

> *Who knoweth one? I, saith Israel, know one: One is God, who is over heaven and earth.*
> *Who knoweth two? I, saith Israel, know two: there are two tables of the covenant; but One is our God, who is over heaven and earth.*
> *Who knoweth three? I, saith Israel, know three: there are three patriarchs, the two tables of the covenant; but One is our God, who is over heaven and earth.*
>   Etc., etc., etc.
> *Who knoweth thirteen? I, saith Israel, know thirteen: Thirteen divine attributes, twelve tribes, eleven stars, ten commandments, nine months preceding child-birth, eight days preceding circumcision, seven days in the week, six books of the Mishnah, five books of the Law, four matrons, three patriarchs, two tables of the covenant; but One is our God, who is over the heavens and the earth.*

Whether "One only kid" and "Who knoweth One?" originated with the common people and were afterward taken into the Passover service, or *vice versa*, is a matter of some doubt. Simrock (*Die deutschen Volkslieder*, p. 520) says that "Who knoweth One?" was originally a German peasants' drinking-song; that it was changed by the monks into an ecclesiastical song, very similar to the form in which we know it; and that afterward, probably during the latter half of the 16th century, it suffered a further adaptation and found a place in the Passover service of the German Jews. "Ehad Mi Yodea"—to give it its Hebrew title—has, however, since been found in the Avignon ritual as a festal table-song for holy-days in general, so that its inclusion in the Jewish Passover service may have been earlier than Simrock surmised. It appears that to the early manuscript Jewish prayer-books it was customary to append popular stories and ballads. That may have been the case with the two songs in question, in which event it is easy to see how they may gradually have been absorbed into, and have become, an integral part of the service itself.

The Rev. A. A. Green, in *The revised Hagada*, expresses the opinion that both of these accumulative songs are essentially Hebrew nursery-rhymes, and he regrets "that they have ever been regarded as anything else." He quotes the first verse of the Scottish "Song of Numbers:"

> *We will all gae sing, boys.*
> *Where will we begin, boys?*
> *We'll begin the way we should*
> *And we'll begin at ane, boys.*

The literature on the subject is a very large one. Those who are interested in the matter should consult the articles "Ehad Mi Yodea" and "Had Gadya" in the *Jewish Encyclopædia* (volumes v and vi), where many authorities are quoted.

It will be noticed that all the Christian forms of the song stop at the number twelve. It has been suggested that the Hebrew version was purposely extended to thirteen, the unlucky number, in order that the Jew might be able to feel that with him thirteen was a holy and, therefore, lucky number.

Like many accumulative songs, "The Ten Commandments" is a most interesting one to listen to. The best folksingers combine their musical phrases in a different manner in each verse, and in so doing display no little ingenuity. Their aim, no doubt, is to compound the phrases so as to avoid the too frequent recurrence of the full-close. I should have liked to have shown exactly how the singer sang each verse of the song, but this would have entailed printing every one of the twelve verses, and consideration of space forbade this. I have, however, given the last verse in full, and this, I hope, will be some guide to the singer.

A form of this song, "Green grow the rushes, O," is known at Eton, and is printed in *English County Songs* (p. 158); and Sullivan introduced a version into *The Yeomen of the Guard*.

No. 98. *The Tree in the Wood*

MISS MASON prints an interesting Devon variant in *Nursery Rhymes and Country Songs* (p. 26), and there is another version from the same county in the Rev. S. Baring-Gould's *Songs of the West* (No. 104, 1st ed.). In his note to the latter, Mr. Baring-Gould says that under the name of "Ar parc caer" the song is well known in Brittany (see Luzel's *Chansons Populaires de la Basse Bretagne*). There are also French ("Le Bois Joli") and Danish forms of the song. See, also, the *Journal of the Folk-Song Society* (volume iii, p. 277); *Journal of the Welsh Folk-Song Society* (volume i, p. 40); and *Folk-Songs from Somerset* (No. 93).

The version given here has not been previously published. The tune, which is in the Æolian mode, is a variant of "Come all you worthy Christian men" (No. 91).

This is one of the easiest of all accumulative songs, both to learn and to sing, and it may, of course, be lengthened indefinitely, according to the taste and inventive powers of the singer.

No. 99. *The Barley-Mow*

I HAVE a large number of variants of this song, which used to be in great request at Harvest Homes.

Chappell, without giving its origin, prints a traditional version in his *Popular Music* (p. 745), and connects it with one of the Freemen's Songs in *Deuteromelia*. In Bell's *Songs of the Peasantry of England*, two versions of the words are given, one from the West Country, and a Suffolk variant. In a note to the former, it is stated that the song was usually sung at country meetings immediately after the ceremony of "crying the neck," an ancient pagan rite, traces of which still survive in Somerset.

A good singer, proud of his memory, will often lengthen the song to abnormal proportions by halving the drink-measures, half-pint, half-quart, half-gallon, and so on.

No. 100. *One man shall mow my meadow*
ALTHOUGH this is a very popular song and very widely known, and I have recently heard soldiers singing it on the march on more than one occasion, I am unable to give a reference to any published version of it.

Cecil J. Sharp.

One Hundred
ENGLISH
FOLKSONGS

1
HENRY MARTIN

Collected and arranged by
CECIL J. SHARP

Allegro moderato

VOICE

1. There were three broth-ers in mer-ry Scot-land, In
lo!— Hul-lo!— cried Hen-ry Mar-tin, What
no! we won't low-er our lof-ty top-sail, Nor

PIANO

mer-ry Scot-land there were three,——— And they did cast lots which of
makes— you sail so nigh?——— I'm a rich mer-chant ship bound for
bow our-selves un-der your lee,——— And you shan't take from us our

them— should go,— should go,— should go,— should go, And— turn rob-ber all
fair Lon-don Town, Lon-don Town, Lon-don Town, Will— you please for to
rich mer-chant goods, mer-chant goods, mer-chant goods, Nor——— point our bold

cresc.

on the salt sea.——— 2. The lot it fell first up-on Hen-ry Mar-
let me pass by?——— 5. Oh no!— Oh no!— cried Hen-ry Mar-
guns to the sea.——— 8. With broad-side and broad-side and at it they

2
BRUTON TOWN

Collected and arranged by
CECIL J. SHARP

3
THE KNIGHT AND THE SHEPHERD'S DAUGHTER

Collected and arranged by
CECIL J. SHARP

wil - low and the dee.
wil - low and the dee.
wil - low and the dee.
wil - low and the dee.

2. You've
3. O
4 He

5.

She rode till she came to the river's side,
She fell on her belly and swam;
And when she came to the other side
She took to her heels and ran.

6.

She ran till she came to the king's fair court,
She pull-ed at the ring:
There was none so ready as the king himself
To let this fair maid in.

7.

Good morning to you, my pretty maid.
Good morning, sir, said she;
You have a knight all in your court
This day has a-robbed me.

8.

O has he robbed you of your gold,
Or any of your fee?
Or has he robbed you of the rarest branch
That grows in your body?

9.

He has not robbed me of my gold,
Nor any of my fee;
But he has robbed me of the rarest branch
That grows in my body.

10.

Here's twenty pounds for you, he said,
All wrap-ped in a glove;
And twenty pounds for you, he said,
To seek some other love.

11.

I will not have your twenty pounds,
Nor any of your fee;
But I will have the king's fair knight
This day to marry me.

12.

The king called up his merry men all,
By one, by two, by three—
Young William once the foremost was,
But now behind came he.

13.

Accurs-ed be that very hour
That I got drunk by wine,
To have the farmer's daughter here
To be a true love of mine!

14.

If I a farmer's daughter am
Pray leave me all alone;
If you make me a lady of a thousand lands
I can make thee lord of ten.

15.

The dog shall eat the flour you sowed,
And thou shalt eat the bran;
I'll make thee rue the day and hour
That ever thou wast born.

16.

He mounted on his milk-white steed,
And she on her pony grey;
He threw the bugle round his neck
And together they rode away.

17.

The very next town that they came to
The wedding bells did ring;
And the very next church that they came to
There was a gay wedding.

4
ROBIN HOOD AND THE TANNER

Collected and arranged by
CECIL J. SHARP

fel - low art thou? quoth bold Rob - in Hood, And what is thy
thou must have more par - tak - ers in store, Be - fore thou up -

bus - i - ness here? For____ now to be brief, thou dost
stand me in deed; For____ I have a staff, he is

look like a thief, And come for to steal the king's deer,____
made of ground graffe And I war - rant he'll do____ my deed,____

1-4   D.C.

Aye,____ and come for to steal the king's deer.____
Aye,____ and I war - rant he'll do____ my deed.____

ff   D.C.

last verse

too.   11. That thing shall not be, says bold Rob-in Hood, For

he is a he-ro so bold; For___ he has best play'd, he is

mas-ter of his trade And by no man shall he be con-troll'd,___

rall.   *a tempo*

Aye, and by no man shall he be con-troll'd.___

THE WRAGGLE TAGGLE GIPSIES, O!

Collected and arranged by
CECIL J. SHARP

14

po - ny, O! That I may ride and — seek my — bride, Who is
mon - ey, O? What care I for my new wed - ded lord? I'm

gone with the wrag - gle tag - gle gip - sies, O! 5. O —
off with the wrag - gle tag - gle gip - sies, O! 8. Last —

he rode high and — he rode low, He rode through woods and —
night you slept on a goose feath - er bed, With the sheet turn'd down so —

cop - ses too, Un - til he came to an o - pen — field, And
brave - ly, O! And to - night you'll sleep in a cold o - pen field, A -

there he es - pied__ his a - la - dy, O!

long with the wrag - gle tag - gle gip - sies, O!

9. What care I for a goose-feath - er bed, With the sheet turn'd down so__

brave - ly, O? For to - night I shall sleep in a cold o - pen field, A -

long with the wrag - gle tag - gle gip - sies, O!

6
LORD BATEMAN

Collected and arranged by
CECIL J. SHARP

VOICE

Moderato maestoso

p

1. Lord Bate - man was   a
4. The Turk he had   one
7. She took him to   her
10. Now sev - en long years   are

PIANO

p

no -   - ble lord, A no - ble lord of   high de - gree. He shipp'd him-self   all a -
on - ly daugh - ter, The fair - est crea - ture that ev er you'd see. She stole the keys   of her
fa - ther's cel - lar And gave to him   the best of wine. And ev - 'ry health   that she
gone____ and past And four - teen days, well   known to me; She pack - ed up   all her

board a____ great   ship, Some for - eign coun -   - try to   go and see. 2. He
fa - ther's pris -   - on, And swore Lord Bate -   - man she would set free. 5. O,
drank un - to____ him: I wish, Lord Bate -   - man, that you were mine. 8. For
gay____ cloth - ing, And swore Lord Bate -   - man she'd go and see. 11. And

mf

18

chain- ed up   all___   by the___ mid - dle Un - til his life _ was   al - most gone.
give it all   to a   fair young la - dy, If out of pris - on she'll set me free.
well, fare-well   to___   you, Lord Bate-man, I   fear I nev - er shall   see you a-gain.
yes! O yes!   cried the   young proud por - ter, He has just now ta - ken his   young bride in.

13.
You tell him to send me a slice of bread,
And a bottle of the best of wine;
And not forgetting that fair young lady
That did release him when close confined.

14.
Away, away went the young proud porter,
Away, away, away went he,
Until he came to Lord Bateman's chamber,
Down on his bended knees fell he.

15.
What news, what news, my young proud porter?
What news, what news hast thou brought to me?
There is the fairest of all young ladies
That ever my two eyes did see.

16.
She has got rings round every finger;
Round one of them she has got three.
She has gold enough all round her middle
To buy Northumb rland that belongs to thee.

17.
She tells you to send her a slice of bread,
And a bottle of the best of wine;
And not forgetting that fair young lady,
That did release you when close confined.

18.
Lord Bateman then in a passion flew;
He broke his sword in splinters three;
Half will I give of my father's portion
If but Sophia have a-crossed the sea.

19.
O then up spoke the young bride's mother,
Who was never heard to speak so free:
You'll not forget my only daughter
If but Sophia have a-crossed the sea.

20.
I own I made a bride of your daughter;
She's neither the better nor worse for me.
She came to me on a horse and saddle;
She may go back in a coach and three.

21.
Lord Bateman prepared another marriage,
And both their hearts were full of glee.
I will range no more to a foreign country
Now since Sophia have a-crossed the sea.

7
BARBARA ELLEN

Collected and arranged by
CECIL J. SHARP

1. In Scot - land I was born and bred, In Scot - land I was dwell - ing, When a young man on his death - bed lay For the sake of Bar - b'ra El - len.

2. He sent his ser - vant to her house To the place where she was dwell - ing, Say - ing: You must come to my mas - ter's house, If your name is Bar - b'ra El - len.

3. So slow - ly she put on her clothes, So slow - ly she came to him, And when she came to his bed - side, She said: Young man, you're dy - ing.

4. A dy - ing man! O don't say so, For one kiss from you will cure me. One kiss from me you nev - er shall have While your poor heart is break - ing.

5. If__ you look up__ at my bed-head You will see my watch a - hang-ing; Here's
6. If__ you look down at my bed's-foot You will see a bowl a - stand-ing, And
7. As__ I was walk-ing down the fields, I heard some birds a - sing-ing; And
8. As__ I was walk-ing down the lane, I heard some bells a - tol-ling; And

my gold ring__ and my gold chain I__ give to Bar - b'ra El - len.
In it is__ the blood I've shed For the sake of Bar - b'ra El - len.
as they sang__ they seem'd to say: Hard__ heart-ed Bar - b'ra El - len.
as they toll'd__ they seem'd to say: Hard__ heart-ed Bar - b'ra El - len.

9.

As I was walking up the groves
And met his corpse a-coming:
Stay, stay, said she, and stop awhile,
That I may gaze all on you.

10.

The more she gazed, the more she smiled,
Till she burst out a-laughing;
And her parents cried out: Fie, for shame,
Hard hearted Barb'ra Ellen.

11.

Come, mother, come, make up my bed,
Make it both long and narrow;
My true love died for me yesterday,
I'll die for him tomorrow.

12.

And he was buried in Edmondstone,
And she was buried in Cold Harbour;
And out of him sprang roses red,
And out of her sweet briar.

13.

It grew and grew so very high
Till it could grow no higher;
And around the top growed a true lover's knot
And around it twined sweet-briar.

8
LITTLE SIR HUGH

Collected and arranged by
CECIL J. SHARP

23

9
GEORDIE

Collected and arranged by
CECIL J. SHARP

Andante

VOICE

PIANO

1. Come, bri - dle me my
six pret-ty babes that
judge he look - ed
Geor - die hang in

milk - white steed, Come, bri - dle me my___ po - ny, That
I have___ got, The sev - enth lies in my bod - y; I'll
down on___ him And said: I'm sor - ry___ for___ thee. 'Tis
gold - en___ chains. (His crimes were nev - er___ man - - y,) Be -

I may ride to fair Lon-don town To plead for my Geor - die.___
free - ly part with them ev - 'ry one, If you'll spare me the life of Geor - die.___
thine own con-fes - sion hath hang - ed___ thee, May the Lord have mer-cy up - on___ thee.___
cause he came of roy - al___ blood And court-ed a vir - tu-ous la - dy.___

2. And when she en - tered in the __ hall There were
4. Then Geor - die look - ed round the __ court, And
6. O Geor - die stole nor cow nor __ calf And he
8. I wish I were in yon - der __ grove, Where

lords and la - dies __ plen - ty. Down on her knees she
saw his dear - est Pol - ly; He said: My dear, you've
nev - er mur - der'd __ an - y, But he stole six - teen of the
times I have been __ man - y, With my broad sword and my

then did __ fall To plead for the life of Geor - die. __ 3. It's
come too __ late, For I'm con - demn'd al - read - y! __ 5. Then the
king's white steeds And sold them in Bo - hen - ny. __ 7. Let
pis - tol too I'd fight for the life of Geor - die. __

Last time

10
LADY MAISRY

no, your tow-er is not__ fall-ing down, Nor does your bow - er burn; But__

we are a-fraid ere__ you re - turn Your__ la-dy will be dead and gone. 6. Come

sad - dle, sad-dle my milk - white steed, Come sad-dle my po - ny too, That__

I may nei - ther__ eat__ nor__drink Till I come to the old__ cas - tell. 7. Now

11
THE OUTLANDISH KNIGHT

Collected and arranged by
CECIL J. SHARP

fa - ther's gold, And some of your moth - er's fee,_____ And
silk - en things, De - liv - er them up un - to me;_____ I
back to her And bent down o - ver the brim._____ She

mf

two of the best nags from out of the sta - ble, Where there stand thir - ty and
think that they look___ too rich and too gay To rot___ all in the salt
caught him a - round___ the mid - dle so small And bun - dled him in - to the

dim.

three. 3. She mount - ed up - on her milk-white steed, And he on his dap - ple
sea. 6. If I must doff off my silk - en things, Pray turn thy back un - to
stream. 9. He drop - ped high, he drop - ped low, Un - til he came to the

p

mf staccato

10.

Lie there, lie there, you false-hearted man,
Lie there instead of me,
For six pretty maidens hast thou a-drowned here
The seventh hath drown-ed thee.

11.

She mounted on her milk-white steed,
And led the dapple-grey;
She rode till she came to her father's house,
Three hours before it was day.

12.

The parrot hung in the window so high,
And heard what the lady did say:
What ails thee, what ails thee, my pretty lady,
You've tarried so long away?

13.

The king he was up in his bed-room so high,
And heard what the parrot did say:
What ails thee, what ails thee, my pretty Polly,
You prattle so long before day?

14.

It's no laughing matter, the parrot did say,
That loudly I call unto thee;
For the cat has a-got in the window so high,
I fear that she will have me.

15.

Well turn-ed, well turned, my pretty Polly;
Well turned, well turn-ed for me;
Thy cage shall be made of the glittering gold,
And the door of the best ivory.

12
THE COASTS OF HIGH BARBARY

Collected and arranged by
CECIL J. SHARP

pi - rate or man - o' - war, cried we? Blow high!_____ Blow
broad - side, they fought all on the main; Blow high!_____ Blow
cru - el sight and griev - ed us full sore, Blow high!_____ Blow

low!_____ and so_____ sail - ed we._____ O no! I'm not a pi - rate but a
low!_____ and so_____ sail - ed we._____ Un - til at last the fri - gate shot_ the
low!_____ and so_____ sail - ed we._____ To see them all a - drown - ing as_ they

man - o' - war, cried he, A - sail - ing down all on the coasts of
pi - rate's mast a - way. A - sail - ing down all on the coasts of
tried to swim to shore. A - sail - ing down all on the coasts of

First & second times | *Third time*

High Bar - ba - ry. 4. Then
High Bar - ba - ry. 7. For
High Bar - ba - ry.

13
THE CRUEL MOTHER

Collected and arranged by
CECIL J. SHARP

14
THE GOLDEN VANITY

Collected and arranged by
CECIL J. SHARP

15
LORD THOMAS OF WINESBERRY

Collected and arranged by
CECIL J. SHARP

16
THE GREEN WEDDING

Collected and arranged by
CECIL J. SHARP

ral - ly, dal - ly, di - do, ral - ly, dal - ly, day. To my ral - ly, dal - ly, di - do,
ral - ly, dal - ly, di - do, ral - ly, dal - ly, day. To my ral - ly, dal - ly, di - do,
ral - ly, dal - ly, di - do, ral - ly, dal - ly, day. To my ral - ly, dal - ly, di - do,
ral - ly, dal - ly, di - do, ral - ly, dal - ly, day. To my ral - ly, dal - ly, di - do,
ral - ly, dal - ly, di - do, ral - ly, dal - ly, day. To my ral - ly, dal - ly, di - do,

Eight times

Last time

ral - ly, dal - ly, day.
ral - ly, dal - ly, day.
ral - ly, dal - ly, day.
ral - ly, dal - ly, day.
ral - ly, dal - ly, day.

2. There
3. She
4. He
5. He

day.

6.

When he came to the wedding-hall, they unto him did say:
You are welcome, Sir, you're welcome, Sir, where have you spent the day?
He laughed at them, he scorned at them, and unto them did say:
You may have seen my merry men come riding by this way.

‖: To my rally, dally, dido,
  Rally, dally, day. :‖

7.

The Squire he took a glass of wine and filled it to the brim:
Here is health unto the man, said he, the man they call the groom;
Here's health unto the man, said he, who may enjoy his bride —
Though another man may love her too, and take her from his side.

‖: To my rally, dally, dido,
  Rally, dally, day. :‖

8.

Then up and spoke the farmer's son, an angry man was he:
If it is to fight that you come here, 'tis I'm the man for thee!
It's not to fight that I am here, but friendship for to show;
So let me kiss your bonny bride, and away from thee I'll go.

‖: To my rally, dally, dido,
  Rally, dally, day. :‖

9.

He took her by the waist so small, and by the grass-green sleeve,
And he led her from the wedding-hall, of no one asking leave.
The band did play, the bugles sound, most glorious to be seen,
And all the way to Headingbourne Town went the company dressed in green.

‖: To my rally, dally, dido,
  Rally, dally, day. :‖

17
THE BRIERY BUSH

Collected and arranged by
CECIL J. SHARP

pricks my heart so sore;— If I once get out of the bri-e-ry bush, I'll

nev-er get in an-y more.—— 5. O— more.——

The above verses are repeated ad libitum, with the substitution of other relatives, e. g. "mother," "brother," "sister," etc. for "father." The arrival of the "true-love" brings the song to a close as follows:—

5.

O hangman, stay thy hand,
And stay it for a while,
For I fancy I see my true-love a-coming
Across the yonder stile.

6.

O true-love, have you my gold?
And can you set me free?
Or are you come to see me hung
All on the gallows tree?

7.

O yes, I've brought thee gold,
And I can set thee free;
And I've not come to see thee hung
All on the gallows tree.

8.

O the briery bush,
That pricks my heart so sore;
Now I've got out of the briery bush,
I'll never get in any more.

18
LORD RENDAL

Collected and arranged by
CECIL J. SHARP

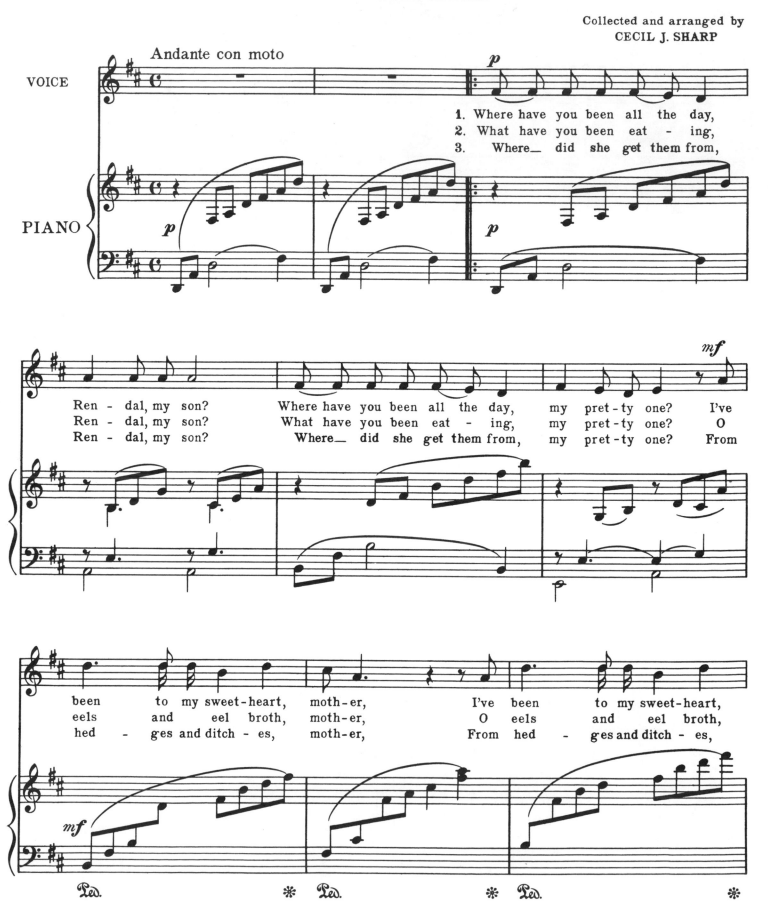

4.

What was the colour on their skin, Rendal, my son?
What was the colour on their skin, my pretty one?
O spickit and sparkit, mother, make my bed soon,
For I'm sick to my heart and I fain would lie down.

5.

What will you leave your father, Rendal, my son?
What will you leave your father, my pretty one?
My land and houses, mother, make my bed soon,
For I'm sick to my heart and I fain would lie down.

6.

What will you leave your mother, Rendal, my son?
What will you leave your mother, my pretty one?
My gold and silver, mother, make my bed soon,
For I'm sick to my heart and I fain would lie down.

7.

What will you leave your brother, Rendal, my son?
What will you leave your brother, my pretty one?
My cows and horses, mother, make my bed soon,
For I'm sick to my heart and I fain would lie down.

8.

What will you leave your lover, Rendal, my son?
What will you leave your lover, my pretty one?
A rope to hang her, mother, make my bed soon,
For I'm sick to my heart and I fain would lie down.

19
BLOW AWAY THE MORNING DEW

Collected and arranged by
CECIL J. SHARP

1. There was a far-mer's son Kept sheep all on the hill; And he walk'd out one May morn-ing To see what he could kill.
2. He look-ed high, he look-ed low, He cast an un-der look; And there he saw a fair pret-ty maid Be-side the wa-t'ry brook.
3. Cast o-ver me my man-tle fair And pin it o'er my gown; And, if you will, take hold my hand, And I will be your own.
4. If you come down to my fa-ther's house, Which is wall-ed all a-round, Then you shall have a kiss from me And twen-ty thou-sand pound
5. He mount-ed on a milk-white steed And she up-on an-oth-er; And then they rode a-long the lane Like sis-ter and like broth-er

And sing blow a-way the morn-ing dew The dew, and the dew.

Blow a-way the morn-ing dew, How sweet the winds do blow.

6.

As they were riding on alone,
They saw some pooks of hay.
O is not this a very pretty place
For girls and boys to play?

Chorus {
And sing blow away the morning dew,
The dew and the dew.
Blow away the morning dew,
How sweet the winds do blow.

7.

But when they came to her father's gate,
So nimble she popped in:
And said: There is a fool without
And here's a maid within.

Chorus. And sing blow away *etc.*

8.

We have a flower in our garden,
We call it Marigold:
And if you will not when you may,
You shall not when you wolde.

Chorus. And sing blow away *etc.*

20
THE TWO MAGICIANS

Collected and arranged by
CECIL J. SHARP

1. O She look'd out of the win-dow as white as an-y milk;— But He look'd in-to the win-dow as black as an-y silk.— Hul-loa, hul-loa, hul-loa, hul-loa, you coal-black smith! you have done me no harm— You nev-er shall change my maid-en name that I have kept so long;— I'd rath-er die a

49

21
THE DUKE OF BEDFORD

Collected and arranged by
CECIL J. SHARP

22
DEATH AND THE LADY

Collected and arranged by
CECIL J. SHARP

Andante sostenuto

VOICE

1. As I walk'd out___ one day, one day, I met an a-ged man___
said: Old man,___ what man are you? What coun-try do you be-
give you gold,___ I'll give you pearl, I'll give you cost-ly rich

PIANO

by___ the way; His head was bald,___ his___ beard___ was gray___ His
long___ un- to? My name is Death; hast___ heard___ of me?___ All
robes___ to wear, If you will spare me a___ lit - tle while,___ And

cloth-ing made of the cold earth-en clay, His cloth-ing made of the cold_earth-en
kings and prin-ces bow down un-to__ me, And you, fair maid,_ must come a-long with
give me time__ my life to a-mend, And give me time__ my life_ to a-

23
THE LOW, LOW LANDS OF HOLLAND

Collected and arranged by
CECIL J. SHARP

1. The ver - y day___ I was mar - ried, That
   Hol - land is___ a___ cold___ place, A
   build my love___ a___ gal - lant ship, A
   moth - er to___ the___ daugh - ter: What___
   not a swaithe goes___ round my waist, Nor a

night I lay on my bed; A press - gang came to___
place where grows no___ green, And Hol - land is___ a___
ship of no - ted___ fame, With four and twen - ty___
makes you to la - ment? O there are lords and___
comb goes in my___ hair, Nei-ther fire - - light___ nor___

my bed - side These words to me___ they said: A -
cold___ place For my love to wan - der in. Though
sea - men bold To___ box her on___ the main. They'll
dukes and squires Can___ ease your heart's con - tent. But___
can - dle - light Can___ ease my heart's des - pair. And___

24
THE UNQUIET GRAVE
or
COLD BLOWS THE WIND

Collected and arranged by
CECIL J. SHARP

1. Cold blows the wind to my true love, And gen-tly drops the rain, I nev-er had but one sweet-heart, And in green-wood she lies slain, And in green-wood she lies slain.

2. I'll do as much for my sweet-heart As an-y young man may; I'll sit and mourn all on her grave For a twelve-month and a day, For a twelve-month and a day.

3. When the twelve-month and one day was past, The ghost be-gan to speak: Why sit-test here all on my grave, And will not let me sleep? And will not let me sleep?

4. There's one thing that I want, sweet-heart, There's one thing that I crave; And that is a kiss from your lil-y-white lips— Then I'll go from your grave, Then I'll go from your grave.

25
THE TREES THEY DO GROW HIGH

Collected and arranged by
CECIL J. SHARP

26
LORD LOVEL

Collected and arranged by
CECIL J. SHARP

61

27
FALSE LAMKIN

Collected and arranged by
CECIL J. SHARP

bolt - ed And the win-dows close pinn'd. 3. At the back kitch - en win - dow False
caught her Right tight in his arm. 7. O spare my life! O_ spare my life! My
fa - ther Come a - rid - ing close by. 11.Dear fa - ther! dear fa - ther! O

Lam - kin crept in; And he prick - ed one of the el - der babes With a bright sil - ver
life that's so sweet; You shall have as man-y bright guin - eas As stones in the
blame not of me; For_ it_ was false_ Lam - kin Mur-der'd ba - by and

pin. 4. O Nurse - maid! O_ Nurse - maid! How sound you do sleep; Can't you
street. 8. O spare my life! O_ spare my life! Till one of the clock; You shall
she. 12.Here's blood in the kitch - en, Here's blood in the hall, Here's_

First & second times | Third time

hear one of those el-der babes A - try - ing to weep? **5.** How
have my daugh-ter Bet - sy, She's the flow'r of the flock. **9.** Fetch
blood in the par - lour, Where the La - dy did fall.

13. False

Lam - kin shall be hung On the gal - lows so high; While his bones shall be

burn - ed In the fire close by.

28
LORD THOMAS AND FAIR ELLINOR

Collected and arranged by
CECIL J. SHARP

Moderato

VOICE

PIANO

p

legato

1. Lord Thom - as he was a bold for - es - ter, And
way___ he flew to fair El - li - nor's bow'r And
rid - dle, my moth - er, come rid - dle, she said, Come
El - li - nor dress'd in her rich___ ar - ray, Her

keep - er of our king's deer;___ Fair El - li - nor she was a gay la - dy, Lord
tin - gled so loud at the ring;___ No one was so read - y as fair El - li - nor To
rid - dle it un - to me;___ Wheth - er I to Lord Thom - as - 's wed - ding shall go, Or
mer - ry men all in green;___ And ev - 'ry town that she rode through They

Thom - as he loved her dear,
let___ Lord Thom - as in.
wheth - er I stay with thee.
took___ her for some queen.

2. Now rid - dle my rid - dle, dear moth - er, said she, And
5. What news,___ what news,___ what news? she cried, What
8. It's hun - dreds are___ your friends, daugh - ter, And
11. She rode till she came to Lord Thom - as - 's house; She

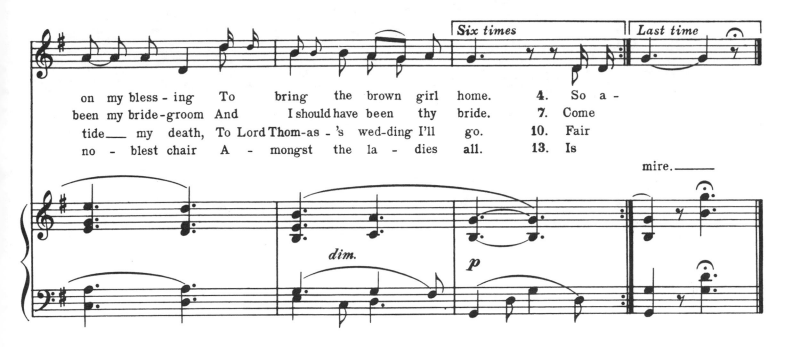

on my bless - ing To bring the brown girl home. 4. So a -
been my bride-groom And I should have been thy bride. 7. Come
tide___ my death, To Lord Thom-as - 's wed-ding I'll go. 10. Fair
no - blest chair A - mongst the la - dies all. 13. Is

mire.___

13.

Is this your bride, Lord Thomas? she said,
    Methinks she looks wonderfully brown;
When you could have had the fairest lady
    That ever trod English ground.

14.

Despise her not, Lord Thomas then said,
    Despise her not unto me;
Fur more do I love thy little finger
    Than all her whole body.

15.

The brown girl had a little penknife,
    Which was both long and sharp;
'Twixt the small ribs and the short she pricked
    Fair Ellinor to the heart.

16.

Oh! what is the matter, Fair Ellen? he said,
    Methinks you look wondrous wan;
You used to have as fair a colour
    As ever the sun shone on.

17.

Oh! are you blind, Lord Thomas? she said,
    Oh! can you not very well see?
Oh! can you not see my own heart's blood
    Come trinkling down my knee?

18.

Lord Thomas he had a sword by his side,
    As he walked through the hall;
He took off the brown girl's head from her shoulders
    And flung it against the wall.

19.

He put the handle to the ground,
    The sword unto his heart.
No sooner did three lovers meet,
    No sooner did they part.

Spoken { *Make me a grave both long and wide,*
And lay fair Ellinor by my side ___
And the brown girl at my feet.

20.

Lord Thomas was buried in the church,
    Fair Ellinor in the choir;
And from her bosom there grew a red rose,
    And out of Lord Thomas the briar.

21.

They grew till they reached the church tip top,
    When they could grow no higher;
And then they entwined like a true lover's knot,
    For all true lovers to admire.

29
THE DEATH OF QUEEN JANE

Collected and arranged by
CECIL J. SHARP

1. Queen Jane was in la-bour For
Hen-ry was a-sent for, King
Jane, my love, Queen Jane, my love, Such a
Hen-ry went mourn-ing And

six days or more, Till her wo-men got tired And wished it were
Hen-ry did come home For to meet with Queen Jane: My love Your eyes do look so
thing was nev-er known, If you have your right side o-pen'd You will lose your dear ba-
so did his men And so did his dear ba-by For Queen Jane did di-

o'er. 2. Good wo-men, good wo-men, Good wo-men if you be, Will you
dim. 4. King Hen-ry, King Hen-ry, King Hen-ry if you be, If you
by. 6. Will you build your love a cas-tle And lie down so deep For to
en. 8. How deep was the mourn-ing How wide were the bands, How

30
FAREWELL, NANCY

Collected and arranged by
CECIL J. SHARP

VOICE

1. Fare - well, my dear - est Nan - cy, since I must now_
3. Your pret - ty lit - tle hands_ can't han - dle our_

PIANO

leave you; Un - to the salt_ seas I_ am bound for to go; But
tack - le, And your pret - ty lit - tle feet on_ our top - mast can't go; And the

let my long ab - sence be_ no trou - ble to you, For_ I shall re -
cold storm - y weath - er, Love, you ne'er can_ en - dure, There - fore, dear - est

turn in the spring, as you know. **2.** Like some pret - ty lit - tle
Nan - cy, to the seas do not go. **4.** So fare - well, my dear - est

sea - boy, I will dress and go with you; In the deep - est of dan - ger, I
Nan - cy, since I must now leave you; Un - to the salt seas I am

shall stand your friend; In the cold storm - y weath - er, when the winds are a -
bound for to go, Where the winds do blow high and the seas loud do

blow - ing, My dear, I shall be will - ing to wait on you then.
roar; So make your - self con - tent - ed; be kind and stay on shore.

31
SWEET KITTY

Collected and arranged by
CECIL J. SHARP

32
THE CRYSTAL SPRING

Collected and arranged by
CECIL J. SHARP

Con espressione

VOICE

PIANO

1. Down   by   some crys - tal
young   men   I

spring   where the night - in - gales sing,   Most   plea - sant it is, in
know,   great   kind - ness will   show,   They will   of - fer   and

sea - son,   to   hear the groves   ring.   Down   by   the riv - er
prof - fer   much   more than   they'll   do;   And when ev - - er   they can

side,   a young cap - tain I es - pi - ed,   En - treat - ing of   his
find   a   maid - en that's   kind,   With   laugh - ing and

true love, for to be ___ his bride. 2. Dear Phyl - lis, ___ says ___ he, can ___
chaff - ing they'll change like the wind: 4. But if e'er I ___ prove ___ false to my

you fan - cy ___ me? All ___ in your soft ___ bow - ers a crown it shall ___
soft lit - tle ___ dove May the o - cean turn ___ des - ert; and the el - e - ments ___

be: You shall take ___ no ___ pain, I ___ will you main - tain, ___ My
move; For wher - ev - er I shall be, I'll be con - stant to thee. ___ Like a

First time *Second time*

ship she's a - load - ed, just ___ come in from Spain. 3. There are
ro - ver ___ I will wan - der and ___ swim through the sea.

33
THE SEEDS OF LOVE

Collected and arranged by
CECIL J. SHARP

Four times | **Fifth time**

small birds so sweet - ly sing. 2. My
flow-'rs that I love so dear. 3. The
those I re-fused all three. 4. The
vow'd that I would wait till June. 5. In
gain - ed the will - low - - - tree.

6. The wil - low-tree will

p *p*

twist And the wil - low-tree will twine,— I oft-en-times have wish'd I were in

mf

that young man's arms That once had the heart of mine, That

cresc. *p*

once had the heart of mine. 7 Come, all you false young men, Do not

leave me here to com - plain:_____ For the grass that has oft - en - times been

tram - pled un - der foot, Give it time, it will rise up a - gain, Give it

time, it will rise up a - gain.

34
THE SPRIG OF THYME

Collected and arranged by
CECIL J. SHARP

rue it is a flour-ish-ing thing, It___ flour-ish-es by night and by
wil-low, wil-low tree it will twist, And the wil-low, wil-low tree___ it will

day; So be-ware___ of a young man's flat-ter-ing tongue, He will
twine; And___ so it was that young and___ false-heart-ed man When he

steal your thyme a-way, a-way, He will steal your___ thyme a-
gain-ed this heart of mine, of mine, When he gain-ed this heart of___

way. 3. I sow-ed my gar-den full of
mine. 6. O thyme it is a pre-cious, pre-cious

35
THE CUCKOO

Collected and arranged by
CECIL J. SHARP

Andante dolente

VOICE

PIANO

1. O the cuc-koo she's a

pret-ty bird, she— sing-eth as she flies. She— bring-eth good tid-ings, she— tell-eth no—

lies. She— suck-eth white flow-ers, for to keep her voice clear; And the

more she—sing-eth cuc-koo, the sum-mer draw-eth near.

2. As___ I was a- walk-ing and a- talk-ing one___ day, I
3. I___ wish I were a schol-ar and could han- dle the___ pen, I would

met my own___ true___ love, as___ he came that___ way. O to
write to my___ lov- er and to all___ ro - ving men. I would

meet him was a plea - sure, though the court -ing was a woe, For___ I
tell them of the grief and woe, that at - tend___ on their___ lies, I___ would

found him___ false - heart - ed,___ he would kiss___ me and go.
wish them___ have___ pi - ty___ on the flow - er when it dies.

D.S. al Fine

36
BLACKBIRDS AND THRUSHES

Collected and arranged by
CECIL J. SHARP

2. The black-birds and thrush-es sang in the green
4. When Jim-my re-turn'd with his heart full of

bush-es; The wood-doves and larks seem'd to mourn for this maid; And the
burn-ing, He found his dear Nan-cy all dead in her grave He

song that she sang was con-cern-ing her lov-er: O Jim-my will be
cried: I'm for-sa-ken, my poor heart is break-ing, O would that I

mf

colla voce

First time **Second time**

slain in the wars I'm a-fraid.
nev-er had left this fair maid!

dim.

rall.

37
THE DROWNED LOVER

Collected and arranged by
CECIL J. SHARP

2. As he was a - sail - ing from his own dear shore, Where the waves and the
4. And all in the church-yard these two were laid, And a stone for re -

bil - lows so loud - ly do roar, I said to my true Love: I shall
mem-brance was laid on her grave: My joys are all end - ed, my

see you no more, So fare - well, my dear - est, you're the
pleas - ures are fled, This grave that I lie in is my

lad I a - dore.
new mar-ried bed.

3. She

Last time

38
THE SIGN OF THE BONNY BLUE BELL

Collected and arranged by
CECIL J. SHARP

1. As I was a-walking one morning in Spring To hear the birds whistle and the nightingale sing, I heard a fair damsel, so sweetly sang she; Saying:
2. I stepp'd up to her and thus I did say: Pray tell me your age and where you belong. I belong to the sign of the Bonny Blue Bell; My
3. Sixteen, pretty maid, you are young for to marry, I'll leave you the other four years for to tarry, You speak like a man without any skill; Four
4. On Monday night when I go there To powder my locks and to curdle my hair, There were three pretty maidens for me awaiting, Saying:
5. On a Tuesday morning the bells they shall ring And three pretty maidens so sweetly shall sing: So neat and so gay is my golden ring, Saying:

39
O WALY, WALY

Collected and arranged by
CECIL J. SHARP.

Andante con espressione

VOICE

PIANO

1. The wa-ter is
wide, I can-not get o'er And nei-ther have I wings to
hand in-to one soft bush, Think-ing the sweet-est flow'r to
plant-ed, O there it grows, It buds and blos-soms like some
ship sail-ing on the sea, She's load-ed deep as deep can

fly. O go and get me some lit-tle boat To car-ry o'er my true love and
find. I prick'd my fin-ger to the bone, And left the sweet-est flow'r a-
rose; It has a sweet and a pleas-ant smell, No flow'r on earth can it ex-
be, But not so deep as in love I am; I care not if I sink or

rall. *a tempo*

1.
2. A-down in the mead-ows the oth-er day, A-gath-'ring
lone. 4. I lean'd my___ back up a-gainst some oak, Think-ing it
cel. 6. Must I be___ bound, O, and she go free! Must I love
swim. 8. O love is___ hand-some and love is fine, And love is

flow'rs, both fine and gay, A-gath-'ring flow-ers, both red and blue, I lit-tle
was a trust-y___ tree. But first he___ bend-ed and then he broke, So did my
one that does not love me! Why should I___ act such a child-ish part, And love a
charm-ing when it is___ true; As it grows old-er it grow-eth cold-er And fades a-

Three times *Last time*

thought what love could do. 3. I put my___
love prove false to___ me. 5. Where love is___
girl that will break my___ heart. 7. There is a___
way like the morn-ing___ dew.

più rall. *a tempo* *morendo*

40
GREEN BUSHES

Collected and arranged by
CECIL J. SHARP

morn - ing __ in __ Spring, For to hear the birds whis - tle and the night - in - gales
fine silk - en __ gownd, I will buy you fine pet - ti-coats with the flounce to the
sir, if you __ please; Come __ let us be go - ing from be - neath the green

sing, I __ saw a young dam - sel, so sweet - ly __ sang __
ground, If __ you will prove loy - al and con - stant __ to
trees, For my true Love is com - ing down yon - der __ I __

she: __ Down __ by the Green Bush - es he thinks to __ meet me.
me __ And for - sake your own true Love, I'll be mar - ried __ to thee.
see, __ Down __ by the Green Bush - es, where he thinks to __ meet me.

2. I step-ped up to her and thus I did say: Why
4. I want none of your pet-ti-coats and your fine silk-en shows: I
6. And when he came there and he found she was gone, He

wait you, my fair one, so long by the way? My true Love, my
nev-er was so poor as to mar-ry for clothes; But if you will prove
stood like some lamb-kin, for - ev - er un - done; She has gone with some

true Love, so sweet-ly sang she, Down by the Green Bush-es he
loy - al and con stant to me I'll for - sake my own true Love and get
oth - er, and for - sak - en me, So a - dieu to Green Bush - es for -

thinks to meet me. 3. I'll
mar - ried to thee. 5. Come
ev - er, cried he.

41
BEDLAM

Collected and arranged by
CECIL J. SHARP

Allegretto teneroso

VOICE

PIANO

1. A - broad as I was walk - ing one morn - ing in the
love he'll not come near me to hear the moan I

Spring, I heard a maid in Bed - lam so sweet - ly she did sing; Her
make, And neith - er would he pi - ty me if my poor heart should break; But,

chains she rat - tled in her hands, and al - ways so sang she.
though I've suf - fer'd for his sake, con - tent - ed will I be, For I

love my love be - cause I know he first loved me.
love my love be - cause I know he first loved me.

42
THE BOLD FISHERMAN

Collected and arranged by
CECIL J. SHARP

Allegretto con grazia

VOICE

PIANO

1. As I walk'd out one May morn-ing Down by the riv - er -
he un-braced his morn-ing-gown, And gen-tly laid it

side, There I be-held a bold fish-er-man Come roll-ing down the
down; When she be-held three chains of gold Went trin-kling three times

tide. 2. Bold fish-er-man, bold fish-er-man, How come you fish - ing
round. 5. Down on her bend-ded knees she fell, Cry-ing: Par-don, par - don

43
THE RAMBLING SAILOR

Collected and arranged by
CECIL J. SHARP

bid you a-dieu, No more to the sea will I go with you; I'll
will you do? Here's ale and wine and bran-dy too; Be -
town I went, To court young maid-ens I was bent; And

trav-el the coun-try through and through, And I'll be a ram-bling
sides a pair of new silk shoes, To trav-el with a ram-bling
mar-ry none was my in-tent, But live a ram-bling

First and second times | *Last time*

sail - or. 2. If
sail - or. 3. The
sail - or.

44
DABBLING IN THE DEW

Collected and arranged by
CECIL J. SHARP

1. O where are you go-ing to, my pret-ty lit-tle dear, With your
what is your fa - ther, my pret-ty lit-tle dear, With your
I should chance to kiss you, my pret-ty lit-tle dear, With your
will you be con - stant, my pret-ty lit-tle dear, With your

red ro-sy cheeks, and your coal-black hair? I'm go - ing a - milk - ing, kind
red ro-sy cheeks, and your coal-black hair? My fa - ther's a farm - er, kind
red ro-sy cheeks, and your coal-black hair? The wind may take it off a - gain, kind
red ro-sy cheeks, and your coal-black hair? That I can - not prom-ise you, kind

sir, she an-swer'd me, And it's dab-bling in the dew makes the milk-maids fair.
sir, she an-swer'd me, And it's dab-bling in the dew makes the milk-maids fair.
sir, she an-swer'd me, For it's dab-bling in the dew makes the milk-maids fair.
sir, she an-swer'd me, For it's dab-bling in the dew makes the milk-maids fair.

2. O
4. And
6. O
8. Then

may I go with you, my pret-ty lit-tle dear, With your red ro-sy cheeks, and your
what is your moth-er, my pret-ty lit-tle dear, With your red ro-sy cheeks, and your
say, will you mar-ry me, my pret-ty lit-tle dear, With your red ro-sy cheeks, and your
I won't__ mar-ry you, my pret-ty lit-tle dear, With your red ro-sy cheeks, and your

coal - black hair? O you may go with me, kind sir, she an-swer'd me, For it's
coal - black hair? My moth-er's a dair-y-maid, kind sir, she an-swer'd me, And it's
coal - black hair? O yes, if you please,____ kind sir, she an-swer'd me, For it's
coal - black hair? No-bod-y ask'd you, kind sir, she an-swer'd me, And it's

dab-bling in the dew makes the milk-maids fair.
dab-bling in the dew makes the milk-maids fair.
dab-bling in the dew makes the milk-maids fair.
dab-bling in the dew makes the milk-maids fair.

Last time

3. And
5. If
7. O

45
THE SAUCY SAILOR

Collected and arranged by
CECIL J. SHARP

VOICE

Andante grazioso

PIANO

1. Come, my dear - est, come, my fair - est, Come and
rag - ged, love, you are dirt - y, love, And your
heard those words come from him, On her
cross the bri - ny o - cean. Where the

tell un - to me, Will you pit - y a poor
clothes they smell of tar. So be - gone, you sau - cy
bend - ed knees she fell. To be sure, I'll wed my
mead - ows they are green; Since you have had the

sail - or - boy, Who has just come from sea? 2. I can
sail - or - boy, So be - gone, you Jack Tar! 4. If I'm
sail - or, For I love him so well. 6. Do you
of - fer, love, An - oth - er shall have the ring. 8. For I'm

46
FANNY BLAIR

Collected and arranged by
CECIL J. SHARP

47
ARISE, ARISE

Collected and arranged by
CECIL J. SHARP

moth - er too, she will quick - ly hear. Go, tell your tales un - to some oth - er, And__
nim - bly step - ped right out of bed And put his__head out of the win - dow__ Poor__
John - ny he__ shall go to sea; And you may write your love a let - ter, And__

whis - per soft ly in her ear. 3. I
John - ny dear was quick - ly fled. 5. Turn
he may read it in Bo-ta-ny Bay 7. O to my grave.

7.

O father, father, pay down my fortune-
It's fifty thousand bright pounds, you know-
And I will cross the briny ocean,
Go where the stormy winds do blow.

8.

O daughter, you may ease your own mind,
It's for your sweet sake that I say so;
If you do cross the briny ocean,
Without your fortune you must go.

9.

O daughter, daughter, I'll confine you;
All in your private room alone;
And you shall live on bread and water,
Brought once a day and that at noon.

10.

I do not want your bread and water,
Nor anything that you may have;
If I can't have my heart's desire,
Then single I'll go to my grave.

48
SEARCHING FOR LAMBS

Collected and arranged by
CECIL J. SHARP

journey to___ pursue? Your pretty lit-tle feet___ they___
pleas-ant is___ the air, I'd rath--er rest on a

tread so sweet, Strike off the morn-ing dew. 3. I'm go-ing to feed my
true love's breast Than an-y oth-er where. 6. For I am thine, and

fa-ther's flock, His young and ten-der lambs, That o-ver hills and
thou art mine; No man shall un-com-fort thee; We'll join our hands in___

o-ver dales Lie wait-ing for___ their dams. 4. O
wed-ded bands And a mar-ried we will be.

Last time

49
GREEN BROOM

Collected and arranged by
CECIL J. SHARP

1. There was an old man and he lived in the West And his
   Jack he did rise and did sharp-en his knives, And he
   John he came back, and up-stairs he did go, And he

trade was a-cut-ting of broom, green broom; He had but one son and his
went to the woods cut-ting broom, green broom, To mar-ket and fair, cry-ing
en-ter'd that fair la-dy's room, her room. Dear John-ny, said she, O can

name it was John, And he li-ed a-bed till 'twas noon, bright noon, And he
ev-'ry-where: O fair maids, do you want an-y broom, green broom? O fair
you fan-cy me, Will you mar-ry a la-dy in bloom, in__ bloom? Will you

li-ed a-bed till 'twas noon. 2. The old man a-rose and un-to his son goes, And he
maids, do you want an-y broom? 4. A la-dy sat up in her win-dow so high, And she
mar-ry a la-dy in bloom? 6. Then John gave con-sent and un-to the church went, And he

p *sostenuto*

swore he'd set fire to his room, his room, If he would not rise and un-
heard John-ny cry-ing green broom, green broom; She rung for her maid and un-
mar-ried this la-dy in bloom, in bloom. Said she: I pro-test there is

but-ton his eyes, And a-way to the woods for green broom, green broom, And a
to her she said: O go fetch me the lad that cries broom, green broom, O go
none in the West Is so good as the lad who sells broom, green broom, Is so

cresc.

f

First and second times | *Last time*

way to the woods for green broom. 3. Then
fetch me the lad that cries broom. 5. Then
good as the lad who sells broom.____

rall.

dim.

p

p

50
THE BONNY LIGHTER-BOY

Collected and arranged by
CECIL J. SHARP

Allegretto grazioso

VOICE

PIANO

1. It's_ of a brisk_ young sail - or lad, And
in my fa - ther's gar - den, Be -

he a pren - tice bound; ___ And she a mer-chant's daugh - ter, With fif - ty thou - sand
neath the wil - low tree, ___ He took me up all in his arms, And kiss'd me. ten - der -

pound ___ They loved each oth - er dear - ly, In sor - row and in joy: ___ Let him
ly ___ Down on the ground we both sat down, And talk'd of love and joy: ___ Let him

go where he will, he's my love still, He's my bon - ny light - er - boy. ___
say what he will, he's my love still, He's my bon - ny light - er - boy. ___

2. 'Twas

3. Her fa-ther, he be-ing near her, He heard what she did say___ He
cried: Un-ru-ly daugh-ter, I'll send him far a-way;___ On
board a ship I'll have him press'd, I'll rob you of your joy:___ Send him
where you will, he's my love still, He's my bon-ny light-er-boy.___

51
THE SWEET PRIMÉROSES

Collected and arranged by
CECIL J. SHARP

Andante espressivo

PIANO

mf   *dim.*   *p*

p Play three times

1. As I____ was a-walk - ing one mid - sum-mer morn - ing, A - view-ing the
2. With three long____ steps I____ stepp'd up____ to her, Not know - ing____
3. I said: Pret - ty maid, how____ far are you go - ing? And what's the oc -

mead - ows and to take the air, 'Twas down by the banks of the sweet prim-é -
her____ as she pass'd me by; I stepp'd up____ to her,____ think - ing to
ca - sion of____ all your grief? I'll make you as hap - py as an - y____

mf

ro - ses, When I____ be - held a most love - ly Fair.
view - her, She ap - pear'd to____ me____ like some vir - gin bride.
la - dy, If you____ will grant____ me one small re - lief.

cresc.   *dim.*

52
MY BONNY, BONNY BOY

Collected and arranged by
CECIL J. SHARP

Andante affettuoso

Now once I was court-ed by a bon-ny, bon-ny boy,— I loved him, I vow and pro-test; I loved him so— well, so ver-y, ver-y well, That I built him a— bow'r in my breast, _____ That I built him a— bow'r in my breast. Now up the green

val - ley and down the long al - ley, Like one that was trou - bled in

mind, I call'd and I did hoot and play'd up - on my lute, But no

bon - ny, bon - ny boy could I find,_____ But no

bon - ny, bon - ny boy could I find. Now I look-ed

east__ and__ I__ look- ed west Where the sun it shone won-der-ful warm, But

who should I__ spy but my bon - ny, bon-ny boy, He was lock'd in an -

oth - er girl's arms,_____ He was lock'd in an -

oth - er girl's arms. Now the girl that's the joy____ of my

bon - ny, bon-ny boy, ___ I'm sure she is nev - er to blame; Though

man - y a long night she has robb'd me of my rest, She nev - er shall

do it a - gain ___ She nev - er shall

do it a - gain.

53ª
AS I WALKED THROUGH THE MEADOWS

(FIRST VERSION)

Collected and arranged by
CECIL J. SHARP

1. As I walk'd thro' the mead-ows to take the fresh air, The
3. Said I: Pret-ty maid-en, shall I go with you To the
5. And when we a-rose from the green moss-y bank, To the

flow-ers were bloom-ing and gay;____ I heard a fair dam-sel so
mead-ows to gath-er some may?____ O no, sir, she said, I would
mead-ows we wan-der'd a - way;____ I pla - ced my love on a

sweet-ly a-sing-ing, Her cheeks like the blos-som in May.____ 2. Said
rath-er re-fuse, For I fear you would lead me a-stray.____ 4. Then I
prim-e-rose bank While I pick'd her a hand-ful of may.____ 6. Then

colla voce

I: Pret - ty maid - en and how came you here In the mead-ows this morn - ing so
took this fair maid by the lil - y - white hand; On the green moss - y bank we sat
ear - ly next morn - ing I made her my bride, That the world might have noth - ing to

mf

soon?____ The maid she re - plied: For to gath - er some may, For the
down,____ And I pla - ced a kiss on her sweet ro - sy lips, While the
say;____ The bells they did ring and the birds they did sing, And I

colla voce

trees they are all in full bloom.____
small birds were sing - ing a - round.____
crown'd her the sweet Queen of May.____

a tempo

cresc.

dim.

53 ♭
AS I WALKED THROUGH THE MEADOWS
(SECOND VERSION)

Collected and arranged by
CECIL J. SHARP

123

54
ERIN'S LOVELY HOME

Collected and arranged by
CECIL J. SHARP

that is ver-y well known, But cru-el-ly he ban - ish'd me from
with me you will roam, We'll bid a - dieu to all our friends in
both set off to roam, A - think - ing we'd got safe a - way from

E - rin's love - ly home.
E - rin's love - ly home.
E - rin's love - ly home.

4.

But when we got to Belfast, 'twas at the break of day,
My true love she got ready a passage for to pay;
Five hundred pounds she did pay down, saying: That shall be your own,
And never mourn for the friends you've left in Erin's lovely home.

5.

But of our great misfortune I mean to let you hear;
'Twas in a few hours afterwards her father did appear.
He marched me back to Armagh gaol, in the county of Tyrone,
And there I was transported from Erin's lovely home.

6.

And now when I heard my sentence it grieved my heart full sore;
And parting from my sweetheart it grieved me ten times more.
I'd seven links all on my chain, and every link a year,
Before I could return again to the girl I loved so dear.

7.

But when the rout came to the gaol to take us all away,
My true love she came on to me, and this to me did say:
Bear up your heart, don't be dismayed, for it's you I'll never disown
Until you do return again to Erin's lovely home.

55
THE TRUE LOVER'S FAREWELL

Collected and arranged by
CECIL J. SHARP

56
HIGH GERMANY

Collected and arranged by
CECIL J. SHARP

2. O Har - ry, dear Har - ry, you mind what I do say, My
3. I'll buy you a horse, my Love, and on it you shall ride, And

feet they are so ten - der I can - not march a - way, And be-
all of my de - light shall be rid - ing by your side; We'll

sides, my dear - est Har - ry, though I'm in love with thee. I
call at ev - 'ry ale - house, and drink when we are dry, So

am not fit for cru - el wars in High Ger - man - y.
quick - ly on the road, my Love, we'll mar - ry by and by.

4. O curs - ed were the cru - el wars that ev - er they should rise And

out of mer - ry_ Eng - land press man - y a lad_ like - wise! They_

press'd young Har - ry_ from me, like - wise my broth-ers three, And sent them to the

cru - el wars in High_ Ger - man - y.

57
SWEET LOVELY JOAN

Collected and arranged by
CECIL J. SHARP

* The measures vary in length.   The time-unit is the quarter-note which is constant in value.

no - ble knight, he___ rode with speed; All mount - ed on his
out he pull'd his___ purse of gold, And said Fair maid, do
then he made her a sol - emn vow, He'd wed her if she

milk - white steed; He rode, he rode, him - self___ a - lone, Un -
this be - hold! All this I'll give if me___ you'll wed. Her
would or no; But this he said to fright - en Joan, As

Four times | **Last time**

til he came to love - ly Joan. 3. Good
cheeks they blush'd like ro - ses red. 5. O
she sat milk - ing all a - lone. 7. Give

7.

Give me the gold, sir, into my hand,
And I will be at your command;
For that will be more good to me
Than twenty husbands, sir, said she.

8.

As he was looking across the mead,
She mounted on his milk-white steed.
He called, he called, 'twas all in vain;
She never once looked back again.

9.

She did not feel that she was safe
Until she reached her true love's gate.
She'd robbed him of his steed and gold,
And left him an empty purse to hold.

10.

It pleased her lover to the heart
To think how well she'd played her part:
To-morrow morning we'll be wed,
And I will be the knight instead.

58
MY BOY WILLIE

Collected and arranged by
CECIL J. SHARP

2. O can she brew and can she bake, My boy Wil-lie?__ O
4. O how old is she now, My boy Wil-lie?__ O

can she brew and can she bake? Wil-lie, won't you tell me now? She can brew and
how old is she now? Wil-lie, won't you tell me now? Twice six,

she can bake, And she can make a wed-ding cake; But she is too young To be
twice sev'n, Twice twen-ty and e-lev'n; But she is too young To be

ta-ken from her mam-my.__
ta-ken from her mam-my.__

3. O

59
WHISTLE, DAUGHTER, WHISTLE

Collected and arranged by
CECIL J. SHARP

hap - py I____ should be;   For I'm young and mer - ry and al - most wear - y Of
not the case with me;   For I'm young and mer - ry and al - most wear - y Of
fills my heart with fear;   For it is a bur - den, a heav - y bur - den, It's
fills my heart with fear.   For it is a bur - den, a heav - y bur - den, It's

my vir - gin - i - ty._____
my vir - gin - i - ty._____
more than I can bear._____
more than I can bear.

5.

Whistle, daughter, whistle,
And you shall have a man.
      (Whistles)   or { I cannot whistle, mother,
You see how well I can.   { But I'll do the best I can.
You nasty, impudent jade,
What makes you whistle now?
O, I'd rather whistle for a man
Than either sheep or cow.

6.

You nasty, impudent jade,
I will pull your courage down;
Take off your silks and satins,
Put on your working-gown.
I'll send you to the fields
A-tossing of the hay,
With your fork and rake the hay to make,
And then hear what you say.

7.

Mother, don't be so cruel
To send me to the field,
Where young men will entice me
And to them I may yield.
Fa, mother it's quite well known
I am not too young grown,
And it is a pity a maid so pretty
As I should live alone.

60
MOWING THE BARLEY

Collected and arranged by
CECIL J. SHARP

1. A Law-yer he went out one day, A - for to take his pleas - ure, And
2. The Law-yer he went out next day, A - think - ing for to view her; But she
3. This Law-yer had a use - ful nag, And soon he o - ver - took her; He
4. Hold up your cheeks, my fair pret - ty maid, Hold up your cheeks, my hon - ey, That

who should he spy but some fair pret - ty maid, So hand - some and so clev - er?
gave him the slip and a - way___ she went, All o - ver the hills to her fa - ther. Where
caught her a - round the mid - dle so small, And on his horse he placed her.
I may give you a fair pret - ty kiss And a hand - ful of gold - en mon - ey.

are you go-ing to, my pret-ty maid, Where are you go-ing, my hon - ey? Go-ing

o - ver the hills, kind sir, she said, To my fa -ther a -mow-ing the bar - ley.

5.

O keep your gold and silver too,
   And take it where you're going;
For there's many a rogue and scamp like you,
   Has brought young girls to ruin.
Where are you going to, *etc.*

6.

Then the Lawyer told her a story bold,
   As together they were going,
Till she quite forgot the barley field,
   And left her father a-mowing.
Where are you going to, *etc.*

7.

And now she is the Lawyer's wife,
   And dearly the Lawyer loves her,
They live in a happy content of life;
   And well in the station above her.
Where are you going to, *etc.*

61
I'M SEVENTEEN COME SUNDAY

Collected and arranged by
CECIL J. SHARP

7. And now she is the sol-dier's wife; And sails a-cross the brine O! The drum and fife is my de-light, And a mer-ry man is mine, O! With my rue dum day, fol the did-dle dol, Fol the dol, the did-dle dum the day.

THE LARK IN THE MORN

Collected and arranged by
CECIL J. SHARP

1. As I was a-walking one morning in the Spring, I met a young damsel, so sweetly she did sing; And as we were a-walking these words she did say:—There's no life like a plough-boy's all in the month of May.

2. The lark in the morn she will rise up from her nest, And mount in the air with the dew all on her breast; And like the pretty plough-boy she will whistle and sing, And at night she'll return to her own nest back again.

63
HARES ON THE MOUNTAINS

Collected and arranged by
CECIL J. SHARP

I were but a young man, I'd soon go a - hunt - ing, To my
I were but a young man, I'd go and bang those bush - es, To my
I were but a young man, I'd go and swim af - ter, To my

right fol___ did - dle de - ro, To my right fol did - dle dee.
right fol___ did - dle de - ro, To my right fol did - dle dee.
right fol___ did - dle de - ro, To my right fol did - dle dee.

Last time

64
O SALLY, MY DEAR

Collected and arranged by
CECIL J. SHARP

Sal - ly, my dear, but your cheek I could kiss it. O__ Sal - ly, my dear, but your
las - sies were black-birds and__ las - sies were thrush-es, If__ las - sies were black-birds and__
wo - men were ducks and__ swum round the wa - ter. If the wo-men were ducks and__

cheek I could kiss it. She laugh'd and re - plied: It you did would you miss it?
las - sies were thrush-es, How soon the young men would go beat - ing the bush - es! Sing
swum round the wa - ter The men would turn drakes and would soon fol - low af - ter.

fal the did - dle i do, Sing whack fal the did - dle day.

65
GENTLY, JOHNNY, MY JINGALO

Collected and arranged by
CECIL J. SHARP

Jin - ga - lo. **2.** I said: You know I love you, dear, Fair maid is a

Jin - ga - lo. **4.** I kiss'd her lips like ru – bies red, Fair maid is a

Jin - ga - lo. **6.** I took her to the church next day, Fair maid is a

lil - y, O! She whis – per'd soft – ly in my ear: Come to me

lil - y, O! She blush'd; then ten – der – ly she said: Come to me

lil - y, O! The birds did sing, and she did say: Come to me

qui - et - ly, Do not do me in – ju – ry; Gen – tly, John – ny, my

qui - et - ly, Do not do me in – ju – ry; Gen – tly, John – ny, my

qui - et - ly, Do not do me in – ju – ry; Gen – tly, John – ny, my

First and second times Last time

Jin - ga - lo.

Jin - ga - lo. **3.** I

Jin - ga - lo. **5.** I

66
THE KEYS OF CANTERBURY

Collected and arranged by
CECIL J. SHARP

5.

O Madam, I will give to you
A little golden bell,
To ring for all your servants
And make them serve you well,
If you will be my joy, my sweet and only dear,
And walk along with me, anywhere.

6.

I shall not, Sir, accept of you
A little golden bell,
To ring for all my servants
And make them serve me well.
I will not be your joy, your sweet and only dear,
Nor walk along with you, anywhere.

7.

O Madam, I will give to you
A gallant silver chest,
With a key of gold and silver
And jewels of the best,
If you will be my joy, my sweet and only dear,
And walk along with me, anywhere.

8.

I shall not, Sir, accept of you
A gallant silver chest,
A key of gold and silver
Nor jewels of the best.
I will not be your joy, your sweet and only dear,
Nor walk along with you, anywhere.

9.

O Madam, I will give to you
A broidered silken gownd,
With nine yards a-drooping
And training on the ground,
If you will be my joy, my sweet and only dear,
And walk along with me, anywhere.

10.

O Sir, I will accept of you
A broidered silken gownd,
With nine yards a-drooping
And training on the ground:
Then I will be your joy, your sweet and only dear,
And walk along with you, anywhere.

67
MY MAN JOHN

Collected and arranged by
CECIL J. SHARP

she will be your bride, your joy and your dear, And she will take a walk with you an - y -

where.

(He)

1. O Mad-am, I will give to you a lit-tle grey - hound, And
2. O Mad-am, I will give to you a fine__ i-v'ry comb, To
3. O Mad-am, I will give to you a cush-ion full of pins, To
4. O Mad-am, I will give to you the keys__ of my heart, To

cresc.   più rall. f   a tempo p   p

ev - 'ry hair up-on its back shall cost a thou-sand pound, If__ you will be my bride, my joy and my dear, And
fas - ten up your sil-ver locks when I am not at home, If__ you will be my bride, my joy and my dear, And
pin __ up your lit-tle ba-by's white mus-e-lins, If__ you will be my bride, my joy and my dear, And
lock it up for-ev-er that we nev-er more shall part, If__ you will be my bride, my joy and my dear, And

mf

152

68

O NO, JOHN!

Collected and arranged by
CECIL J. SHARP

4.

O Madam, I will give you jewels;
I will make you rich and free;
I will give you silken dresses.
Madam, will you marry me?
  O No, John! No, John! No, John! No!

5.

O Madam, since you are so cruel,
And that you do scorn me so,
If I may not be your lover,
Madam, will you let me go?
  O No, John! No, John! No, John! No!

6.

Then I will stay with you for ever,
If you will not be unkind.
Madam, I have vowed to love you;
Would you have me change my mind?
  O No, John! No, John! No, John! No!

69
THE BRISK YOUNG BACHELOR

Collected and arranged by
CECIL J. SHARP

4. Home come I both wet and wear - y, No dry clothes for
5. If I scarce - ly make an an - swer, She will say: O
6. Lis - ten, all you brisk young bach - e - lors! If that you would

to put on, But right up-stairs and down in the cel - lar With the ket - tle
come! come! come! The wom - en say they will have pleas - ure; Poor man's work is
hap - py be, When you want some one to live with you Think of what has

p staccato

mf marcato

I must run.
nev - er a - done. } With my whack fal lor, the did - dle and the di - do,
come to me. }

f

Whack fal lor, the did - dle - i - day.

mf

f

70
RUGGLETON'S DAUGHTER OF IERO

Collected and arranged by
CECIL J. SHARP

Moderato

VOICE

PIANO

1. There was a man lived in the West; Fal lal lal lal lal lal li - do, He
   if your din - ner you must have, Fal lal lal lal lal lal li - do, Then
   you shall brew and you shall bake, Fal lal lal lal lal lal li - do, And

mar - ried a wife—she was not of the best; She was Rug-gle-ton's daugh-ter of I - e - ro.
get it your-self; I am not your slave, Said Rug-gle-ton's daugh-ter of I - e - ro.
you shall make your_ white hands black To_ Rug-gle-ton's daugh-ter of I - e - ro.

2. Said he, when he came in from plough: Fal lal lal lal lal li - do, Ho!
4. For I won't brew and I won't bake, Fal lal lal lal lal li - do, And
6. He took a stick down off the rack; Fal lal lal lal lal li - do, And

71
WILLIAM TAYLOR

Collected and arranged by
CECIL J. SHARP

72
SWEET WILLIAM

Collected and arranged by
CECIL J. SHARP

VOICE / **PIANO**

Andante

p e legato *p*

1. A— sail - or's life— is a
   had not sail - ed far
   kneel - ed down and she

mer - ry life. He'll rob young girls of their heart's de - light, Then
on the deep Be - fore a king's ship she chanced to meet. O
wrote a song, She wrote it neat and she wrote it long; At

cresc.

go and leave them to sigh and moan— No tongue can tell— when he
all you sail - ors come tell me true, Is my sweet Wil - liam on
ev - 'ry line, O, she shed a tear, And at the end:— Fare you

73
THE WATCHET SAILOR

Collected and arranged by
CECIL J. SHARP

through your long ab-sence she's going to be wed. To - mor - row in Bris - tol this
know I was sol-emn - ly· prom – ised to you. The sail – or's my true love, and

cresc.

wed-ding's to be____ And I am in - vit - ed the same for to see. 3. Jack
I'll be his bride; There's none in this world I can fan - cy be – side. 6. Then the

mf *cresc.* *f*

went and got li - cence the ver - y same night, And walk'd in - to
tail - or, he roar'd like a man that is mad, I'm ru – in'd, I'm

mf

Bris - tol as soon as 'twas light. He sat in the Tem - ple church -
ru - in'd, I'm ru - in'd, he said. All you that have sweet-hearts, take

cresc.

yard for a while Till he saw the bride com - ing, which caused Jack to
them while you may,__ Or else the Jack Tars, they will take them a -

f   *cresc.*

smile.   4. He
way.

ff

74
SCARBOROUGH FAIR

Collected and arranged by
CECIL J. SHARP

1. Where are you go-ing? To Scar - bo-rough Fair? Pars - ley, sage, rose - ma - ry and thyme, Re - nem - ber me to a bon - ny lass there, For once she was a true

3. Tell her to wash it in yon - der well, Pars - ley, sage, rose - ma - ry and thyme, Where wa - ter ne'er sprung nor a drop of rain fell, And she shall be a true

5. Tell her to plough it with one ram's horn, Pars - ley, sage, rose - ma - ry and thyme, And sow it all o - ver with one pep - per - corn, And she shall be a true

75
BRIMBLEDON FAIR
OR, YOUNG RAMBLE-AWAY

Collected and arranged by
CECIL J. SHARP

1. As I was a-rid-ing to Brim-ble-don Fair, I saw pret-ty Nan-cy a-curd-ling her hair, I gave her a wink and she roll'd a dark eye, And said I to my-self: I'll be

3. I said: Pret-ty Nan-cy, don't laugh in my face, But she an-swer'd by slip-ping a-way from the place. So to find her I ram-bled thro' fair Lin-coln-shire, And I vow'd I would ram-ble, I

there by and by.
did not care where.

2. I watch'd and I watch'd, all the
4. Come all you young maid-ens, wher-

night in the dark,
ev - er you be,

For to ask pret - ty Nan - cy to
And ask find pret - ty Nan - cy and

be my sweet-heart. But all that she said, when I saw her next day: And are
bring her to me. And all you young ram-blers you mind and take care, Or

cresc. molto

you the young rogue they call Ram - ble - a - way?
else you'll get brim-bled at Brim - ble - don Fair.

76
BRIDGWATER FAIR

Collected and arranged by
CECIL J. SHARP

1. All you who roam, both young and old, Come lis-ten to my sto - ry bold. For miles a-round from far and near__ They come to see the rigs o' the fair. O Mas-ter John, do you be-ware! And don't go kiss-ing the girls at Bridg - wa-ter fair.

lads and lass - es they come through From Stow-ey, Sto-gur-sey and Can-ning-ton too. That far - mer from Fid-ding - ton, true as my life,__ He's come to the fair to look for a wife. O Mas - ter John, do you be-ware! And don't go kiss-ing the girls at Bridg - wa-ter fair.

Tom and Jack, they look so gay, With Sal and Kit they haste a - way To shout and laugh and have a spree,_ And dance and sing right mer - ri - ly. O Mas - ter John, do you be-ware! And don't go kiss-ing the girls at Bridg - wa-ter fair.

First and second times

2. The
3. There's

Third time

4. The jo-vial plough-boys all se-rene, They dance the maid-ens on the green. Says
car-rot-ty Kit so jol-ly and fat, With her girt flip-pe -ty, flop-pe-ty hat; A
up with the fid-dle and off with the dance, The lads and lass-es gai - ly prance, And

John to Ma - ry: Don't you know— We won't go home till morn - ing O? O
hole in her stock-ing as big as a crown, And the hoops of her skirt hang-ing down to the ground. O
when it's time to go a - way They swear to meet a - gain— next day. O

Mas - ter John, do you be -ware! And don't go kiss-ing the girls at Bridge-
Mas - ter John, do you be -ware! And don't go kiss-ing the girls at Bridge-
Mas - ter John, do you be -ware! And don't go kiss-ing the girls at Bridge-

First and second times | *Last time*

wa - ter fair.
wa - ter fair.
wa - ter fair.

5. There's
6. It's

77

THE CRABFISH

Collected and arranged by
CECIL J. SHARP

she fell a-sick, O, and all her wish Was just to put her lips to a
fish-er-men, O fish-er-men, O come and tell me Have you a lit-tle crab-fish you
caught him and bought him and clapt him on a dish: O wife put thy lips to this
8. Hey man and ho man, come hith-er do ye hear? But the crab-fish was read-y and

lit-tle crab-fish. Mash-a row dow dow dow did-dle all the day, Mash-a
can sell me? Mash-a row dow dow dow did-dle all the day, Mash-a
lit-tle crab-fish. Mash-a row dow dow dow did-dle all the day, Mash-a
caught him by the ear. Mash-a row dow dow dow did-dle all the day, Mash-a

row dow dow dow did-dle all the day.
row dow dow dow did-dle all the day.
row dow dow dow did-dle all the day.
row dow dow dow did-dle all the day.

78
THE BEGGAR

Collected and arranged by
CECIL J. SHARP

Allegro ma non troppo

VOICE

1. I'd just as soon be a
2. I've six-pence in my pock-et and I've
3. Some-times we call at a
4. Some-times we lie like

PIANO

beg-gar as a king, And the rea-son I'll tell you for why;   A
work'd hard for it, Kind land-lord, here it is.   Nei-ther
no-ble-man's hall, And beg for bread and beer;   Some-
hogs in a stye With a flock of straw on the ground;   Some-

king can-not swag-ger, nor drink like a beg-gar, Nor be half so hap-py as
Jew nor Turk shall make me work, While beg-ging is as good as it
times we are lame, some-times we are blind, Some-times too deaf to
times eat a crust that has roll'd in the dust, And are thank-ful if that can be

79
THE KEEPER

Collected and arranged by
CECIL J. SHARP

Jack-ie, boy! Sing ye well! Hey down, der - ry, der - ry down, A -

SECOND VOICE

Mas-ter! Ver-y well! Ho down, A -

mong the leaves so— green, O! To my hey down, down, Hey down,

mong the leaves so— green, O! To my ho down, down, Ho down,

mf

f *p* *p* *cresc.*

D.S. Last time

der-ry, der-ry down, A - mong the leaves so— green, O.

A - mong the leaves so— green, O.

Last time

f *dim.* *rall.* *p*

80
THE THREE SONS

Collected and arranged by
CECIL J. SHARP

3. The stout mil-lard he stole the corn, The spin - ner he stole yarn, And the
4. The mil-lard he was drown'd in his pond, The spin-ner was hang'd by his yarn, And the

tail - or went forth and he stole broad-cloth For to keep those three scamps
dev - il ran a - way with the tail - or one day With the broad-cloth un - der his

warm,___ For to keep those three scamps warm. And the tail - or went forth and he
arm,___ With the broad-cloth un-der his arm. And the dev - il ran a - way with the

stole broad-cloth For to keep those three scamps warm.
tail - or one day With the broad-cloth un - der his arm.

non legato

81
JACK HALL

Collected and arranged by
CECIL J. SHARP

VOICE

Moderato

PIANO

1. O my name it is Jack Hall, chim-ney-
twen-ty pounds in store, that's no
tell me that in gaol I shall
rode up Ty-burn Hill in a
lad-der I did grope, that's no

sweep, chim-ney - sweep, O my name it is Jack
joke, that's no joke, I have twen-ty pounds in
die, I shall die, O they tell me that in
cart, in a cart, O I rode up Ty - burn
joke, that's no joke, Up the lad - der I did

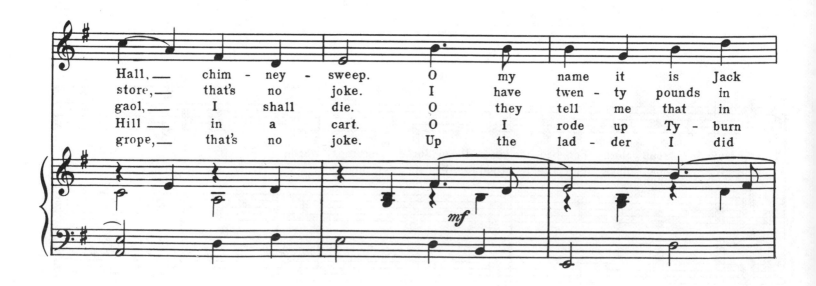

Hall, chim-ney - sweep. O my name it is Jack
store, that's no joke. I have twen-ty pounds in
gaol, I shall die. O they tell me that in
Hill in a cart. O I rode up Ty - burn
grope, that's no joke. Up the lad - der I did

82
DRIVING AWAY AT THE SMOOTHING IRON

Collected and arranged by
CECIL J. SHARP

smooth-ing-iron, She stole my heart a - way,_____ And driv-ing a - way at the
smooth-ing-iron, She stole my heart a - way,_____ And driv-ing a - way at the
smooth-ing-iron, She stole my heart a - way,_____ And driv-ing a - way at the

1-3

smooth-ing - iron, She stole my heart__ a - way._____
smooth-ing - iron, She stole my heart__ a - way._____
smooth-ing - iron, She stole my heart__ a - way._____

4. 'Twas on a Thurs - day morn - ing When I be-held my dar - ling; O
5. 'Twas on a Fri - day morn - ing When I be-hold my dar - ling; O
6. 'Twas on a Sat-ur-day morn - ing When I be-held my dar - ling; O
7. 'Twas on a Sun - day morn - ing When I be-held my dar - ling; O

she was fair__ and she was free In ev - 'ry high__ de - gree._____ Yes!
she was fair__ and she was free In ev - 'ry high__ de - gree._____ Yes!
she was fair__ and she was free In ev - 'ry high__ de - gree._____ Yes!
she was fair__ and she was free In ev - 'ry high__ de - gree._____ Yes!

83
THE ROBBER

Collected and arranged by
CECIL J. SHARP

Andante maestoso

VOICE

1. When I was eight-een I took a wife; I
fa-ther cried: O, my dar-ling son! My

PIANO

mf   *sfz*   *f*

loved her dear-ly as I loved my life;
wife she wept and cried: I am un-done!
And
My

mf

to main-tain her both fine and gay, I went a-rob-bing, I
moth-er tore her white locks and cried: O, in his cra-dle, O

p   *cresc.*

went a-rob-bing on the King's high-way. I nev-er robb'd an-y
in his cra-dle he should have died! When I am dead and go

poor man yet, And I was nev-er in a trades-man's debt; But I
to my grave, A flash-y fu-ne-ral let me have; Let

robb'd the lords and the la-dies gay, And car-ried home the gold, And
none but bold rob-bers fol-low me, Give them good broad swords, Give

car-ried home the gold to my love straight-way. To Cu-pid's gar-den I
them good broad swords and lib-er-ty. May six pret-ty maid-ens bear

84
JOHN BARLEYCORN

Collected and arranged by
CECIL J. SHARP

VOICE

Moderato e maestoso

PIANO

There were three kings came

from the West, Their vic-to-ry to try; And they have tak-en a

sol-emn oath, John Bar-ley-corn should die. Fol the dol the

did-i-ay,___ Fol the dol the did-i-ay-ge-wo.___

So there he lay for a full fort-night, Till the dew on him did -fall: Then
Bar - ley - corn sprang up a - gain, And that sur - prised them all.
Fol the dol the did - i - ay,— Fol the dol the did - i - ay - ge - wo.
There he re - main'd till

mid - sum - mer, And look'd both pale and wan; Then

Bar - ley - corn he got a beard, And so be - came a

man. Fol the dol the did - i - ay, ___

Fol the dol the did - i - ay - ge - wo. ___

più lento

O Bar-ley-corn is the choi-cest grain That e'er was sown on land; It will do more than an-y grain, By the turn-ing of your hand. Fol the dol the did-i-ay,— Fol the dol the did-i-ay-ge-wo.——

85
POOR OLD HORSE

Collected and arranged by
CECIL J. SHARP

I was young and in my prime And in my sta - ble lay, They
mas - ter used to ride me out And tie me to a stile, And

gave to me the best of corn And the best of clo - ver hay. Poor old
he was court - ing the mil - ler's girl While I could trot a mile. Poor old

horse! Poor old mare! _____
horse! Poor old mare! _____

2. My

86
BOTANY BAY

Collected and arranged by
CECIL J. SHARP

1. Come, all young men of learn-ing good, A__ warn-ing__ take by
char-ac-ter was ta - ken, And__ I was__ sent to

me. I'll__ have you quit night-walk - ing And shun bad com-pa-
gaol. My__ par-ents tried to__ clear__ me But noth-ing would pre-

ny; I'll__ have you quit night-walk-ing Or else you'll rue__ the__
vail. 'Twas__ at our Rut-land ses - sions The Judge to me__ did__

day, And you will be trans-port - ed And__ go__ to__ Bo-ta-ny Bay. 2. I
say: The Ju-ry's found you guilt - y, You must go__ to__ Bo-ta-ny Bay. 4. To

was brought up in Lon - don town, A — place I — know full well; Brought
see my poor old fa - - ther As — he stood at the bar; Like -

up by hon - est par - ents, The truth to you I'll tell. Brought up by hon - est
wise my dear old moth - er Her old gray locks she tore. And in tear-ing of her

par - ents, Who loved me ten - der - ly, Till I be - came a
old gray locks These words to me she did say: O son! O son! what

1.
rov - ing blade To — prove my — des - ti - ny. 3. My
2.
hast thou done? Thou art bound for — Bo - ta - ny Bay.

87
ADMIRAL BENBOW

Collected and arranged by
CECIL J. SHARP

88
BOLD NELSON'S PRAISE

Collected and arranged by
CECIL J. SHARP

fought like a he - ro till he died A - mid the bat - tle go - ry. But the

marcato

day was won, their line was broke, While all a - round was lost in smoke, And

Nel - son he got his death-stroke. That's the man For old Eng-land! He

faced his foe with his sword in hand And he lived and he died in his glo - ry.

cresc. *f* *ff colla voce*

89.
SPANISH LADIES

Collected and arranged by
CECIL J. SHARP

chan - nel of old Eng - land: From U - shant to Scil - ly is

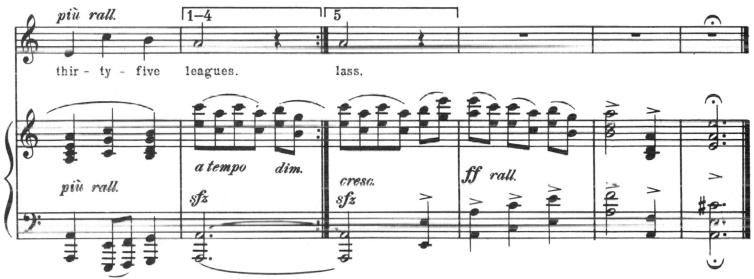

thir - ty - five leagues. lass,

4.

Then the signal was made for the grand fleet to anchor,
And all in the Downs that night for to lie;
Let go your shank painter, let go your cat stopper!
Haul up your clewgarnets, let tacks and sheets fly!

5.

Now let ev'ry man drink off his full bumper,
And let ev'ry man drink off his full glass;
We'll drink and be jolly and drown melancholy,
And here's to the health of each true-hearted lass.

Chorus. We will rant and we'll roar like true British sailors,
We'll rant and we'll roar all on the salt seas,
Until we strike soundings in the channel of old England:
From Ushant to Scilly is thirty-five leagues.

90
THE SHIP IN DISTRESS

Collected and arranged by
CECIL J. SHARP

1. Ye sea-men bold that plough the o-cean, See
   dan-gers lands-men nev-er know, 'Tis for no hon-our nor pro-mo-tion, No
   tongue can tell what they un-der-go. There's blus-t'rous wind, and the heat of bat-tle, Where

   rats and mice, how they did eat them, Their
   hun-ger for to ease, we hear. And in the midst of all their tri-als Captain and men bore an e-qual share. At last there came a scant up-on them, A

ing was left these poor souls to cher-ish; For want of food they are fee-ble grown,__Poor
free to die, but,___ mess-mate-broth-ers, Let some-one up to the top-mast stay___And

mf   *p*

1.

fel-lows, they will__ sure-ly per-ish, They're wast-ed now to skin and bone. 3. The
see what there he__ can dis-cov-er, Whilst I un-to the

p   *p*

non legato

2.

Lord do pray. 5. I think I see a__ ship a-sail-ing, Come__

legato

non legato

bear-ing down with some re-lief. As soon as this glad__

cresc.

91
COME ALL YOU WORTHY CHRISTIAN MEN

Collected and arranged by
CECIL J. SHARP

1. Come all you worth-y Christian men, That dwell up-on this land, Don't spend your time in ri-ot-ing: Re-mem-ber you're but man. Be watch-ful for your lat-ter end; Be read-y when you're call'd. There are ma-ny chan-ges in this world; Some

all you worth-y Christian men, That are so ver-y poor, Re-mem-ber how poor La-za-rus Lay at the rich man's door, While beg-ging of the crumbs of bread That from his ta-ble fell. The Scrip-tures do in-form us all That in

rise while oth- ers fall. 2. Now, Job he was a_ pa - tient man, The_ rich - est in_ the
heav - en he_ doth dwell. 4. The time, a - las, it_ soon will come When part - ed we_ shall

East: When he was brought to_ pov - er- ty, His sor - rows soon in - creased. He_
be; But_ all the dif - f'rence it will make Is in joy and mis - er - y. And

bore them all most pa - tient- ly; From sin he did re - frain; He al - ways trust- ed_
we must give a strict ac- count Of_ great as well as_ small. Be - lieve me now, dear

in the Lord; He_ soon got rich a - gain. 3. Come
Chris - tian friends, That God will judge us all.

92
WASSAIL SONG

Collected and arranged by
CECIL J. SHARP

1. Was - sail and was - sail _____ all o - ver the

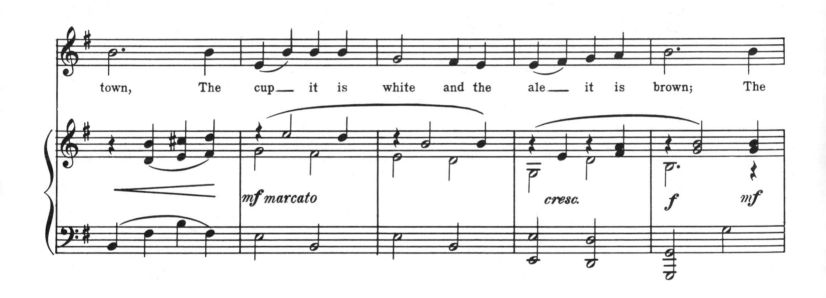

town, The cup __ it is white and the ale __ it is brown; The

cup __ it is made of the good old ash - en tree, And so is our

IT'S A ROSEBUD IN JUNE

Collected and arranged by
CECIL J. SHARP

1. It's a rose-bud in June and vio-lets in full bloom, And the small birds sing-ing love-songs on each spray; We'll pipe and we'll sing, Love, We'll dance in a ring, Love, When each lad takes his lass all on the green grass; And it's

all _____ to plough__ Where the fat ox - en graze low, And the

lads and the lass - es to__ sheep-shear - ing go.

2. When__ we have a - shear'd all our jol - ly, jol - ly

sheep, What__ joy can be great - er than to talk of their in - crease?

We'll_ pipe and we'll sing,_Love, We'll_ dance in a ring,_Love, When each

lad takes his lass All_ on the green grass; And it's all_____ to

plough_ Where the fat ox - en graze low, And the lads and the lass - es to_

sheep - shear - ing go.

94
A BRISK YOUNG SAILOR

Collected and arranged by
CECIL J. SHARP

down, He takes some strange girl on his knee And he tells her what he does not tell
see. I wish it'd been the same by me Be - fore I'd gain'd my love's com-pa -

me.   3. Hard grief for me and I'll tell you why, Be-cause that
ny.   6. The green-est field it shall be my bed; A flow-'ry

she has more gold than I. Her gold will waste, her beau-ty pass, And she'll come like
pil - low shall rest my head, The leaves which blow from tree to tree They shall be the

cresc.

dim.

f

dim.

f

me, a poor girl, at last.
cov - er - lets o - ver

1.   2.

1.   me.   2.

p più rall.

95
THE SHEEP-SHEARING

Collected and arranged by
CECIL J. SHARP

month of the year, In the month call - ed June, When the weath - er's too
sheep they're all shorn, And the wool car - ried home, Here's a health to our

hot to be borne, The mas - ter doth say, As he goes on his
mas - ter and flock; And, if we should stay, Till the last goes a -

way: To - mor - row my sheep shall be shorn, To - mor - row my
way, I'm a - fraid 'twill be past twelve o' - clock, I'm a - fraid 'twill be

sheep shall be shorn. 3. Now
past twelve o' - clock.

96
THE TWELVE DAYS OF CHRISTMAS

Collected and arranged by
CECIL J. SHARP

*) See Note upon this song in the Preface.

97
THE TEN COMMANDMENTS

Collected and arranged by
CECIL J. SHARP

THE TEN COMMANDMENTS

1. *1st voice*   Come and I will sing to you.
   2nd voice   What will you sing to me?
   1st voice   I will sing one one-e-ry.
   2nd voice   What is your one-e-ry?
   1st voice   One and One is all alone, and evermore shall be so.

2. *1st voice*   Come and I will sing to you.
   2nd voice   What will you sing to me?
   1st voice   I will sing you two-e-ry.
   2nd voice   What is your two-e-ry?
   1st voice   Two and two are lily-white babes a-clothed all in green, O!
   One and One is all alone, and evermore shall be so.

3. *1st voice*   Come and I will sing to you.
   2nd voice   What will you sing to me?
   1st voice   I will sing you three-e-ry.
   2nd voice   What is your three-e-ry?
   1st voice   Three of them are thrivers,
   And two and two are lily-white babes a-clothed all in green, O!
   One and One is all alone, and evermore shall be so.

4. *1st voice*   Come and I will sing to you.
   2nd voice   What will you sing to me?
   1st voice   I will sing you four-e-ry.
   2nd voice   What is your four-e-ry?
   1st voice   Four are gospel makers.
   Three of them are thrivers,
   And two and two are lily-white babes a-clothed all in green, O!
   One and One is all alone, and evermore shall be so.

(The remaining verses are sung after the manner of all cumulative songs, i.e. each verse deals with the next highest number and contains a new line. The additional lines are shown in the last and twelfth verse which follows.)

12. *1st voice*   Come and I will sing to you.
    2nd voice   What will you sing to me?
    1st voice   I will sing you twelve-e-ry.
    2nd voice   What is your twelve-e-ry?
    1st voice   Twelve are the twelve apostles.
    Eleven and eleven are the keys of heaven,
    And ten are the ten commandments.
    Nine are the nine that brightly shine,
    And eight are the eight commanders.
    Seven are the seven stars in the sky,
    And six are the six broad waiters.
    Five are the flamboys under the boat,
    And four are the gospel makers.
    Three of them are thrivers,
    And two and two are lily-white babes a-clothed all in green, O!
    One and One is all alone, and evermore shall be so.

98
THE TREE IN THE WOOD

Collected and arranged by
CECIL J. SHARP

1. All— in a wood there was a tree, And a fun-ny and a cu-rious tree; And the tree was in the wood, And the wood lay down in the val-ley— be-low, And the wood lay down in the val-ley— be-low, be-low.

2. And on this tree there was a bough, And a fun-ny and a cu-rious bough; And the

bough was on the tree, And the tree was in the wood, And the wood lay down in the

D.S.

val-ley___ be - low, And the wood lay down in the val-ley___ be - low, be - low.

D.S.

1.

All in a wood there was a tree,
And a funny and a curious tree;
And the tree was in the wood,
And the wood lay down in the valley below.

2.

And on this tree there was a bough,
And a funny and a curious bough;
And the bough was on the tree,
And the tree was in the wood,
And the wood lay down in the valley below.

3.

And on this bough there was a twig,
And a funny and a curious twig;
And the twig was on the bough,
And the bough was on the tree,
And the tree was in the wood,
And the wood lay down in the valley below.

4.

And on this twig there was a nest,
And a funny and a curious nest;
And the nest was on the twig,
And the twig was on the bough,
And the bough was on the tree,
And the tree was in the wood,
And the wood lay down in the valley below.

5.

And in this nest there was an egg,
And a funny etc.

6.

And in this egg there was a bird,
And a funny etc.

7.

And on this bird there was a head,
And a funny etc.

8.

And on this head there was a feather,
And a funny and a curious feather;
And the feather was on the head,
And the head was on the bird,
And the bird was in the egg,
And the egg was in the nest,
And the nest was on the twig,
And the twig was on the bough,
And the bough was on the tree,
And the tree was in the wood,
And the wood lay down in the valley below.

*) This measure is sung twice in the third verse, three times in the fourth verse, etc. etc.

99
THE BARLEY-MOW

Collected and arranged by
CECIL J. SHARP

O I will drink out of the nip-per-kin, boys; So

here's a good health to the bar-ley-mow. The nip-per-kin and the brown bowl!— So

here's a good health to the bar-ley-mow. O I will drink out of the

pint, my boys, So here's a good health to the bar-ley-mow. The pint, the

nip-per-kin and the brown bowl. So here's a good health to the bar - ley-mow. O

I will drink out of the quart, my boys; So here's a good health to the bar - ley-mow. The

quart, the pint, the nip - per - kin and the brown bowl. ___ So

here's a good health to the bar - ley - mow. O

*) There will be three $\frac{3}{8}$ measures in the next verse, four in the fifth verse, and so on.
These measures must be sung with increasing speed as the song develops.

THE BARLEY-MOW

Solo.   **1.** O I will drink out of the nipperkin, boys;
Chorus.   *So here's a good health to the barley mow.*
           The nipperkin and the brown bowl.
           So here's a good health to the barley mow.

        2. O I will drink out of the pint, my boys;
           So here's a good health to the barley mow.
           The pint, the nipperkin and the brown bowl.
           So here's a good health to the barley mow.

        3. O I will drink out of the quart, my boys;
           So here's a good health to the barley mow.
           The quart, the pint, the nipperkin and the brown bowl.
           So here's a good health to the barley mow.

The song proceeds after the usual manner of cumulative songs, an additional measure being added to each verse. The last verse runs as follows:—

       13. O I will drink out of the clouds, my boys;
           So here's a good health to the barley mow.
           The clouds, the ocean, the sea, the river, the well, the tub, the
              but, the hogshead, the keg, the gallon, the quart, the
              pint, the nipperkin and the brown bowl.
           So here's a good health to the barley mow.

100
ONE MAN SHALL MOW MY MEADOW

Collected and arranged by
CECIL J. SHARP

2.

Three men shall mow my meadow,
Four men shall gather it together,
Four men, three men, two men, one man,
  and one more,
Shall shear my lambs and ewes and rams,
And gather my gold together.

3.

Five men shall mow my meadow,
Six men shall gather it together,
Six men, five men, four men, three men,
  two men, one man, and one more,
Shall shear my lambs and ewes and rams,
And gather my gold together.

(And so on *ad lib.*)

✳) This measure must be played twice in the 2nd verse, three times in the 3rd verse, and so on.